ORLANDO BLOOM

The amazing true story of Britain's hottest new star

ORLANDO BLOOM

THE BIOGRAPHY

A C PARFITT

JB

JOHN BLAKE

Published by John Blake Publishing Ltd,
3, Bramber Court, 2 Bramber Road,
London W14 9PB, England

www.blake.co.uk

First published in paperback in 2004

ISBN 1 84454 061 8

British Library Cataloguing-in-Publication Data:

A catalogue record for this book is available from the British Library.

Design by www.envydesign.co.uk

Printed in Spain by Bookprint

3 5 7 9 10 8 6 4 2

Papers used by John Blake Publishing are natural, recyclable products made from wood grown in sustainable forests. The manufacturing processes conform to the environmental regulations of the country of origin.

All pictures © Rex Features, except p62 © Camera Press / Jerry Watson and p83
Mary Evans Picture Library

For Sarah and Poppy

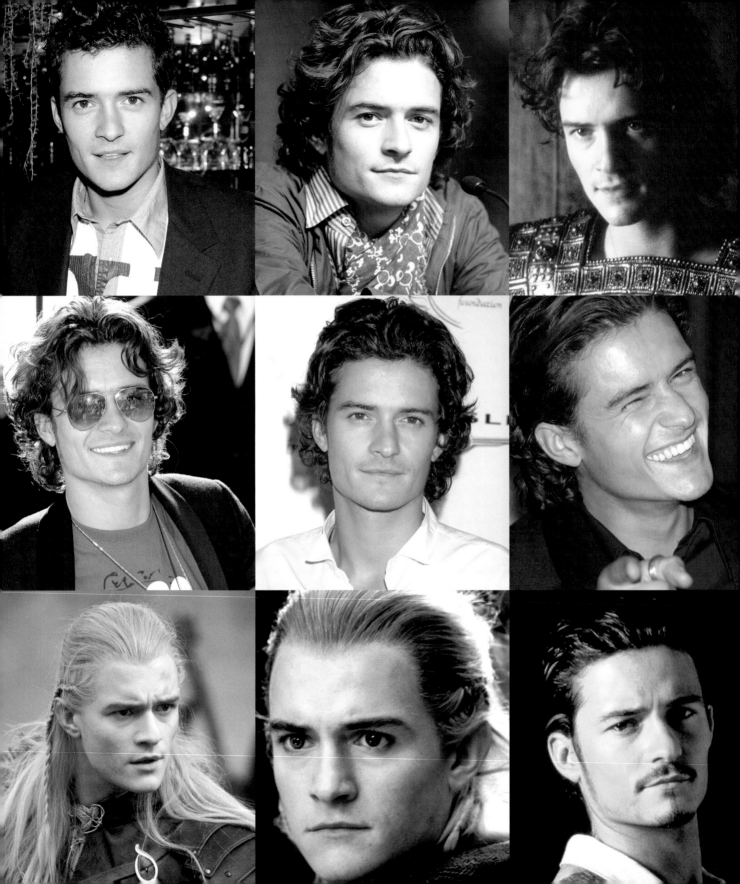

contents

introduction

At 27 years of age Orlando Bloom has achieved more than many aspiring young actors dream of achieving in a lifetime: starring roles in the biggest movies of his – or any other – generation; critical acclaim; and fans in literally every corner of the world. He has been described as a one-man boy band: when he makes a public appearance the screams are invariably deafening. And yet, while undoubtedly he has style, there is substance there as well.

How has he done it? What is it about him that sets hearts fluttering? Well, there's the obvious – model features and boyish good looks always help in Hollywood, and Orlando has them by the barrel load. But you can't hoodwink the punters, and you can't get by in Tinseltown on good looks alone. Orlando has achieved his success with a measure of personal and professional integrity that is somewhat lacking in other stars who could be mentioned.

As I have discovered in writing this book, he is a fiercely private individual who keeps his personal life just that – personal. Not for him the conveniently timed photo shoot in a celebrity magazine. He is not the kind to use his relationship with another famous face to put himself one more rung up the career ladder. And yet he has climbed that ladder with phenomenal speed, always choosing projects that speak to him as an actor rather than as a businessman.

The story of Orlando's life so far is characterised by a judicious mixture of lucky breaks and inspired choices and, if one thing is certain, it is that we will be seeing a great deal more of this young man from Kent who has captured the imagination of his female fans and the admiration of film-goers everywhere.

ONE WHO IS FAMOUS THROUGHOUT THE LAND

'I DON'T KNOW ANY FAMILY THAT DOESN'T HAVE A LITTLE STORY SOMEWHERE. BESIDES, IF YOU DIDN'T HAVE THOSE THINGS IN YOUR LIFE, YOU'D BE SO BLAND.'

The peaceful town of Canterbury in Kent, England, would seem to the casual passer-by an unlikely place for a world-famous political activist to end his days. Tourists flock there in their thousands, of course, to visit the cathedral; while they are there, they might take in the museum of Roman antiquities, or stroll in the perfectly manicured gardens. They certainly wouldn't head there for excitement. It is a small town, quaint some would say, and above all serene. But maybe, after the life he had led, that was exactly what Harry Bloom wanted: a bit of peace and quiet.

His career had, after all, been nothing if not eventful. Born in 1913 to a Jewish Afrikaans family, Harry was educated in South Africa at the University of Witwatersrand. He went on to work as a lawyer, journalist and novelist; it was the novels that got him into trouble. The South Africa in which Harry found himself living was a place of unrest, division and hatred. For most of the 20th century the country had practised a policy of racial segregation, with black people unable to enjoy the same rights as the white minority. In 1947 this policy was given a name – apartheid – and South Africa became, to right-thinking people everywhere, one of the most frowned-upon states in the world.

Harry was a wealthy, influential man, a successful lawyer who seemed to have every chance of becoming a judge. But, if South Africa had been good to Harry Bloom, it was not a regime of which he felt he could be proud. In 1956 he published a novel, *Episode* (later renamed *Transvaal Episode*), which was to change the course of his life for ever.

Transvaal Episode was set in the fictional township of Nelstroom. In 1952 the African National Congress led a campaign of defiance

Canterbury – a quaint small town that fostered a big talent.

against the South African government, and the novel tells the tale of an uprising in the aftermath of this campaign. The inhabitants of the township become educated to the injustice of their situation, and the book exposes the failings and inhumanity of apartheid. 'Facts are twisted,' writes Harry Bloom, 'illusions fostered, truth destroyed to prove that the perverted is normal, the sordid noble, the brutal beautiful, the guilty innocent, the coward a hero, disaster a victory...' If anything was likely to upset the South African government, it was the subversive message of this book.

And upset them it did. The book was banned in South Africa because the authorities believed it had the power to upset race relations and cause major social disturbances across the entire country. They were probably right. South Africa was not a place where freedom of speech was smiled upon. But freedom of speech was something Harry Bloom believed was worth fighting for, and once he had found his voice there was little the authorities could do to stop him, apart from throw him in jail – which is exactly what they did.

What tortures were inflicted on Harry in his cold prison cell, history does not record. Given the South African government's record for such things, they are likely to have been severe. But the spirit of the man could not be dampened, nor could the message of his work. The government encouraged people to organise mass burnings of the book. Their efforts were in vain. Thousands of people managed to hold on to their copies in secret; it sold 20,000 copies in South Africa alone,

> Facts are twisted, illusions fostered, truth destroyed to prove that the perverted is normal, the sordid noble, the brutal beautiful, the guilty innocent, the coward a hero, disaster a victory...'
>
> HARRY BLOOM, *TRANVSAAL EPISODE*

and was exported to 22 countries. It was awarded the British Authors' Club Prize for the best novel of 1956, although Harry was, of course, denied permission by the government to travel to England to collect his award. Instead he threw himself more completely into his work. He completed a second novel, *Whittaker's Wife*, while serving a subsequent detention, and he wrote the libretto for *King Kong: An African Jazz Opera*, which told the tragic story of a boxer from a black ghetto.

Harry worked and was jailed alongside

Nelson Mandela, and became a legendary figure in the anti-apartheid struggle. His life's work was remarkable, and yet the story of the 20th century is filled with such tales of courage over adversity. Twenty years before Harry Bloom finally exiled himself to England, another book had been published which told the story of a struggle against the forces of those who would crush the freedom of the world. It had been written by an academic who had witnessed first-hand the pointless despair of the trenches during the First World War, and who had watched with horror as the power of Nazi Germany rose inexorably. That man was JRR Tolkien; the book, *The Lord of the Rings*.

By 1963 South Africa had become too dangerous a place for Harry Bloom. The violence he was threatened with by those who wanted the status quo to endure was too much to risk. He came to England in an act of self-imposed exile, taking with him his wife Sonia, and found himself living in a rather more sedate environment. He took a position as Professor of Law at the University of Kent, and before long settled in Canterbury.

In Sonia, a language-school teacher, Harry had found a soulmate. Years later, after Harry's death, she would take part in a memorial event at the University. The famous actor and director Sir Richard Attenborough was

Harry Bloom struggled alongside Nelson Mandela in the fight to rid South Africa of apartheid.

present to talk about his film *Cry Freedom*. Set in South Africa, it tells the heart-rending true story of journalist Donald Woods' investigation of the death of his black activist friend Steve Biko. Attenborough revealed that he had originally wanted to make a film of Harry's book *Transvaal Episode* but, when that project failed to materialise, he moved on to *Cry Freedom*. So, had circumstances been different, the Bloom family name would have hit the big screen rather earlier than it eventually did. But what those present at the event would remember most from that day was Sonia's moving tribute to her late husband: her words were a testament to a relationship based on love and mutual respect.

It was into such a relationship that two children were born. Sonia gave birth to a girl, Samantha, in 1975. And on 13 January 1977 she brought a little boy into the world. She named him Orlando, and it was only in hindsight that she would realise the irony of this name: Orlando means 'one who is famous throughout the land'. How could Sonia ever have guessed that one day Orlando would be famous not only throughout the land, but also throughout the world?

The family into which Orlando Bloom was born was an artistic one. He was named after Orlando Gibbons (1583–1625), the leading British composer of his day. Organist of the Royal Chapel, keyboard player to the court of King Charles and Organist of Westminster Abbey, Gibbons produced an impressive body of sacred choral music which is still performed today, and is one of the most influential composers of all time. It says a great deal about Sonia Bloom that she should name her son after such an individual. Orlando's mother was cultured, intelligent and bohemian, and she did her best to ensure that he and his sister were brought up in a creative environment. Sonia Bloom was a free spirit,

and it was this perhaps more than anything that was the overriding influence on the young boy as he grew up. Orlando would later say that she 'pretty much did what the hell she wanted in life, and I intend to do the same'.

Harry died in 1981, when Orlando was just four. Sonia nursed him, helped in this by a close family friend, Colin Stone. Colin, a teacher at the language school where Sonia worked, was an invaluable source of friendship and support to the Bloom family during the final difficult months of Harry's life. After his death, Colin became Orlando's guardian and would be a father figure to the young boy throughout his formative years.

Like everyone's, those formative years had their ups and downs. Orlando struggled in school, not because he was unintelligent – far from it – but because he suffered from dyslexia. This condition – its name comes from Greek and means 'difficulty with words' – affects up to 6 per cent of the population. Its symptoms can vary from individual to individual, but the principal signs of dyslexia in young children are problems with reading and spelling. Only in fairly recent years has dyslexia become a recognised condition. Schools have learned to spot and help children who suffer from it, and people now understand that dyslexic children's difficulty with the written word is not a sign of stupidity, but of something quite different. Had Orlando been born 50 years ago, he would have encountered a quite different attitude: dyslexic children tended to be dismissed as under-performers, whereas often quite the opposite is true. Those with dyslexia frequently turn out to be innovative, lateral thinkers; they have intuitive problem-solving skills; and above all they tend to be very creative individuals.

Orlando was lucky. His mother spotted in him an innate creativity and did everything she could to encourage this trait in her young son. From an early age Orly, as he was known to family and friends alike, found himself performing in all sorts of different forums, from the Bible-reading classes which his mum insisted he attend, to various children's drama groups. Sonia was not discouraged by her son's dyslexia, and even now dismisses it, as keen as ever to highlight his creative side: 'He reads scripts all the time. It hardly affects him now. Orlando got eight O levels and three A levels. He is a wonderful sculptor. Very artistic and very bright.'

Even when he was a child, it seemed that a love of performing ran through young Orlando's blood, though not everything always went according to plan. He later recalled the embarrassment he endured during his first public performance. The venue? A packed-out local theatre in Canterbury. The swashbuckling Orlando Bloom's first role? As a monkey.

In fact, he was one of three monkeys dressed in fake-fur monkey suits, the sort of garment that can make you uncomfortably hot. He was carrying out his theatrical duties with considerable aplomb, when he was struck with an irresistible urge to scratch his bottom. Without thinking – he was only four years old, after all – he did exactly that. It was an innocent enough gesture, and probably not entirely out of character for the role he was playing, but the audience fell about with laughter.

Orlando froze. He forgot what he was supposed to be doing and was struck by overwhelming stage fright. 'It was quite a big deal,' he remembers, and no doubt at that tender age it was. That he still remembers it 20

'My mum pretty much did what the hell she wanted in life, and I intend to do the same.'

ORLANDO BLOOM

years on says much about the effect it had on the young lad. Fortunately, though, his little thespian faux pas was not to cool his love of the stage.

As well as persuading Orly to express his creativity through his own acting skills, Sonia

It was *The A-Team*, among others, that inspired Orlando to tread the boards.

encouraged him in other ways, too. She would regularly take him to the theatre so that he could be exposed to as wide a range of influences as possible; ultimately, however, it was television that inspired the boy to follow his star in the acting world. His favourite shows were classic Saturday-night fare: *The A-Team*, the popular series following the adventures of a maverick group of soldiers on the run from the US Army for a crime they did not commit; and *Knight Rider*, starring David Hasselhoff as the owner of the talking car with a mind of its own. 'As soon as I realised that the heroes on *The A-Team* and *Knight Rider* weren't real,' he explained many years later, 'I

decided I wanted to act because, I thought, I'd love to be any number of those guys.'

Orlando was further encouraged in his acting ambitions at school. He was fortunate enough to be able to attend St Edmund's School in Canterbury. Set among the green fields of St Thomas Hill, the school is adjacent to the University of Kent, where Harry Bloom spent the latter part of his career. His drama teacher, Richard Parsons, has fond memories of how keen Orlando was to appear on the stage. In his final year at St Edmund's he appeared as a singing police sergeant in a production of Gilbert and Sullivan's *The Pirates of Penzance*. For Orly, however, one role was not enough, and he asked if he could also appear as a pirate extra – little knowing that ten years later he would be playing pirates on a slightly grander scale.

'I think that says a lot about Orlando,' says Mr Parsons. 'He was happy to play any role, whether minor or lead, just as long as he was on stage. He had talent, enthusiasm and always stood out. I think it's easy to forget that Orlando was an excellent actor. Even at 14 or 15 he was getting lead roles against people who were 17 or 18. It's easy to think that he's a good-looking chap and that's why he's getting roles in Hollywood, but he was a very good character actor.'

Orlando didn't just like playing pirates on

7

stage – in his teenage years he was starting to resemble one in real life. 'He liked earrings and friendship bracelets,' recalls the drama teacher. 'There were a few battles to try and get him to take them off, because they were against regulations.' It was clearly a battle that Orlando won – to this day he collects trinkets and jewellery almost obsessively.

'He was happy to play any role, whether minor or lead, just as long as he was on stage. He had talent, enthusiasm and always stood out.'

RICHARD PARSONS, ORLANDO BLOOM'S DRAMA TEACHER

If he excelled on the stage, Orly had more trouble in the classroom because of his dyslexia. But St Edmund's was clearly the perfect place for him, and he completed all his courses and passed all his exams to the satisfaction of his teachers, his parents and himself. 'I just had to work harder to get them,' he admitted later. This sense of hard work would prove to be essential in his future career. And it seems that his difficulty with the written word was largely overcome when he found himself writing about something about

which he was truly passionate: 'I enjoy the company of girls,' he once wrote in an English essay, 'and I would like to think that they enjoy mine.'

Given that he displayed his classical good looks even at an early age, there can be little doubt that girls enjoyed the company of the teenage Orlando. But he wasn't always as smooth and confident as he appears today. He later revealed that his first foray into the world of women was not an unqualified success, but then he *was* young enough not to know better: 'My first kiss was terrible. I was 12, and I didn't know what to do with my teeth.' Clearly things improved after that bungled first attempt. After Orlando hit the big time, he appeared on a radio phone-in and was confronted by an old school mate. He remembered the boy in question, but was not prepared for the question he asked: 'Do you remember nicking my girlfriend?'

Unsurprisingly, Orlando was taken aback. 'No,' he replied, 'I don't remember nicking your girlfriend, mate.'

The young lady in question was unavailable for comment.

According to the Chinese calendar, Orlando is a dragon. Among the characteristics of those born under this birth sign are said to be attractiveness and magnetism. As a boy,

'I enjoy the company of girls,'
wrote Orlando, 'and I like to
think that they enjoy mine.'

Orly already possessed those attributes in abundance. He was a popular young man, and modest – he later admitted to being quite embarrassed when he was told by his mother the meaning of his name – and she remembers him as being a very energetic lad. 'Orlando was a very normal boy, full of action, full of ideas, totally and absolutely normal.' The star himself remembers his childhood somewhat differently: 'I was a little bit crazy. Not crazy-crazy, but I was always the first one to jump off the wall or dive into the lake without thinking about the consequences of my actions.'

Was the young Orlando a Will Turner in the making? Perhaps, perhaps not, but if he managed to keep a level head about him as he entered his formative teenage years, credit was due to him. When he was nine years old his mother dropped a bombshell on the young boy which he was to keep a secret from the world for the next 15 years.

Throughout his short life Orly grew up thinking that Harry Bloom – novelist, academic and world-renowned opponent of apartheid – was his father. He had no reason to believe otherwise; this is what his mother had told him for as long as he could remember. Then, one day, his entire perception of his place in the world was turned on its head as Sonia gently explained that Harry was not his biological father after all. Orlando was, in fact, the son of a man who had been a family friend for many years; a man who had been appointed his legal guardian after Harry's death; a man who had taken a truly fatherly interest in the young boy.

Colin Stone was Orlando's real father.

A less well-adjusted person would have found this very difficult news to cope with. But Sonia had always encouraged Orly to be easy-going and broad-minded. He did not allow this startling news to affect him unduly and, when he finally spoke about it to the world, he was at pains to point out that to his family the situation was not a big deal at all. 'My mum was married to one man, but I was fathered by a second. I think she was waiting for me to be old enough to understand it. But when *would* you tell a kid about that stuff? It's very difficult.' Ever the optimist, Orlando managed to view the situation in a positive light. 'I don't know any family that doesn't have a little story somewhere. Besides, if you didn't have those things in your life, you'd be so bland.'

Far from having an adverse effect on the family, Sonia's revelation seemed to bring them closer. Colin felt nothing but pride for the two children and their achievements and, in the context of that supportive and loving family, Orlando was able to concentrate on the future. And what a future it would turn out to be…

CHAPTER TWO

WILDE THING

'IT WAS AN AMAZING PARTY SCENE WITH EVEN MORE AMAZINGLY BEAUTIFUL WOMEN. IT WAS A MIXED GAY CROWD, TRANSVESTITES, GO-GO GIRLS, JUST A WHOLE LOAD OF NIGHT CREATURES.'

As Orlando approached the age of 16 it became more and more clear to him that, if he wanted to follow the career that seemed to be in his very blood, Canterbury was not the place to do it. It was too limiting, too restricting, and the opportunities for the young man to gain the experiences he would need if he was to mature into a fine and distinctive leading actor were simply not to be found there. He began to set his sights further afield, and there seemed to him to be only one place he could go that could offer him what he wanted: London. So he finished his studies at St Edmund's and, with his mother's blessing and like Dick Whittington of old, went to the capital to seek his fortune.

There were other reasons for moving to London. Orlando's best friend had recently moved there to go to university, which made Canterbury seem an even less attractive place to stay. To the teenage star-in-the-making, London must have seemed like a whole different world, laden with opportunities ripe for plucking. Orlando was very young, very free and very single, and he fully intended to have a very good time. Despite this, he never lost his focus. He hadn't decided to leave school at 16 and fritter his life away: he was moving away from Canterbury for a very specific reason. 'I finished my education in London,' he would later explain, and in doing so he showed all the enthusiasm and determination to become an actor that his drama teacher had spotted while he was still at school.

He did not arrive aimlessly. The National Youth Theatre had put him on a scholarship, which enabled him to study and practise the acting that he loved so much. The National Youth Theatre was formed in 1956 and gives people between the ages of 13 and 21 an opportunity to become involved in theatre. It doesn't just take aspiring actors, but also welcomes those who want to be involved behind the scenes.

Orlando, however, only wanted to tread the boards. He wanted to take advantage of the fact that he could start to learn how to act to a professional standard, from professionals, and then perform in proper theatres in London and elsewhere across the country. And he cannot have been oblivious to the fact that the National Youth Theatre had been a hotbed of superstardom. Not only had one of Orlando's all-time acting heroes, Daniel Day-Lewis, started his career there, it had also been the launching pad for performers of the calibre of Ben Kingsley, Derek Jacobi, David Suchet and Timothy Dalton. To have been offered a scholarship put Orlando on the first rung of his ladder to

Orlando thrived at the National Youth Theatre, as did one of his all-time acting heroes Daniel Day-Lewis.

success, and he fully intended to exploit it for all it was worth.

Ed Wilson was Artistic Director of the National Youth Theatre at the time Orlando arrived, and he remembers the teenager's abilities vividly. He was, recalls Wilson, 'one of the finest young performers we've ever had in our companies, in all of the 15 years I've been in the post.' Even at 16, Orlando was already turning heads.

He was as keen as he could have been to make the most of his opportunity. But all work and no play would have made Orlando a very dull boy indeed, and that was certainly not a trap into which the young actor

intended to fall. Orlando Bloom had been let loose on London, and was all set to enjoy the party.

But, for all his intentions to live life in the capital to the full, it was not the case that Orlando found Swinging London swinging from the moment he arrived. 'I moved to London expecting to meet a whole bunch of new mates instantly,' he admits. When those mates did not immediately materialise, he discovered what so many people discover when they first move to the sprawling mass of humanity that is London: 'It can be such a lonely city at first.' At least he had a means of meeting people, though, and once he'd made his mark at the National Youth Theatre and

'Orlando was one of the finest young performers we've ever had in our companies.'

ED WILSON, ARTISTIC DIRECTOR, NATIONAL YOUTH THEATRE

found himself a place to live behind the BT Tower – a very desirable, central location – things started to look up.

Without much hesitation Orlando threw himself into something that he enjoyed almost as much as acting: clubbing. 'That was a big growth period for me,' he reflected when looking back on those days. 'Me and my friends, who were mostly older, used to go clubbing, and I experienced a lot because of that.' The teenager found himself in with the beautiful crowd, spending time in fabulously hip London clubs like Kooky, Hollywood Babylon and Billion Dollar Babes, among others. Some of the clubs he frequented at that time had reputations for being hotbeds of drug-taking, but that wasn't the sort of thing he was getting into.

The star-in-the-making was much more interested in the people – especially the girls. 'It was an amazing party scene,' he remembers fondly, 'with even more amazingly beautiful women. It was a mixed gay crowd, transvestites, go-go girls, just a whole load of night creatures.' Orlando was becoming a night creature himself, and why not? He was young, he was beautiful and he knew what he wanted: fun. Like everyone else in the party set he found himself involved with, he knew he could go out to one of these clubs and be a movie star for a night. 'Trust me,' he commented after he had become a real-life star. 'It's much easier faking it.'

When he wasn't living it up in the super-cool clubs and bars of nineties London, the teenager was earning a crust working in clothes shops. It was perhaps here that he developed his love for fashion. He had not always taken such an interest in his clothes, and in fact when he was younger he admitted to paying scant attention to his image. He left all that to his sister, Samantha, who used to make sure her little brother dressed properly. 'She had great style,' he concedes. 'She'd go to Oxfam and come back with a shirt or a suede jacket.'

By the time Orlando came to London, however, he'd moved on from second-hand clothes from Oxfam. The beautiful young things of London needed to be dressed in something finer. To supplement his income, he took jobs in high-class clothing shops like Paul Smith and Boxfresh, the almost unbelievably trendy boutique in London's Covent Garden. Unfortunately, the life of a struggling actor was not one that allowed him to satisfy his desire for the hippest gear. He used to ogle all the latest trainers in the windows of Soho shops: 'I could never afford them, mind. I used to go in every weekend and stare them out.' It was a far cry from the situation he would find himself in a few short years later, when clothing manufacturers would throw their newest lines his way, practically begging him to wear them anywhere he would be photographed.

They were good times for Orlando, and he enjoyed them. But he would later reflect that he was pleased he had, as he put it, 'got all that out of my system'. These days Orlando prefers a quieter life. 'I'm not a big partyer. I feel like I know what partying has to offer and it's not something I need to do any more.'

The British American Drama Academy has

> 'I'm not a **big** partyer. I **feel** like I **know** what **partying** has to offer and it's **not** something I **need** to do any **more.**'
>
> ORLANDO BLOOM

produced some of the world's finest actors. It was founded in London in 1983 to encourage students from all parts of the world to study classical theatre with some of the leading exponents of the art form. In the past, its students have had the privilege of being taught by such renowned names as Kevin Spacey, Jeremy Irons and Alan Rickman. The people who run the British American Drama Academy know talent when they see it. Orlando Bloom was spotted in a National Youth Theatre production and, having completed two seasons, was offered a coveted scholarship to the Academy.

It was an excellent environment to find himself in. Even better was the fact that, having been spotted during auditions, he found himself with an agent. For a working actor, this is the first hurdle that needs to be jumped, as without an agent you have little or no means of being put up for even the smallest jobs. To have been signed up at such a young age was truly a stroke of luck for Orlando. So it was that the young actor landed bit parts on television: they were small roles, but essential in terms of experience. *Casualty* is a popular prime-time TV show which Orlando once described as being 'like *ER*, only cheaper'. He was offered a role as a self-mutilator – a far cry from the more heroic parts that would eventually make his name – and he played the part with quiet skill. He took away from his first screen role as much as he put in, most valuably the confidence to be able to perform in front of the camera.

It was a small part, but it was enough to get him noticed. TV is one thing, but what every aspiring young actor wants is a role in a feature film. In 1997 Orlando hit the silver screen for the first time in the recherché British art-house movie *Wilde*.

The film is an acclaimed biopic of Oscar Wilde, the renowned Victorian novelist, playwright and aesthete. Based on a best-selling biography by Richard Ellman, it stars Stephen Fry as the Irish-born writer, and tells a dramatic and tragic story. Wilde was a talented and exuberant man, whose works such as *The Importance of Being Earnest* and *The Picture of Dorian Gray* assured him a place in the annals of great literature.

He was happily married to the beautiful Constance Lloyd and had two children whom he loved very much. One day, however, he was seduced by a young man and forced to confront the homosexuality that he had been repressing throughout his life. Yet, once he had admitted the truth about his homosexuality to himself, he was hugely liberated, not only in his personal life, but in his work as well. He started a passionate relationship with Lord Alfred 'Bosie' Douglas (played in the film by Jude Law), who, while reciprocating Wilde's affections, also had a predilection for young rent boys. Wilde referred to it as 'the love that dare not speak its name', and it was a desire that he was to learn to share.

When Wilde's homosexuality was exposed, he faced not only public shame, but also imprisonment: it was a crime to be homosexual in Victorian England. Sentenced to two years' hard labour, he was brought almost to death's door by the terrible conditions he went through; and yet it was also a creative time for him, as he penned one of his most famous works, *The Ballad of Reading Gaol*, in prison. On his release, he cut off all ties from Bosie, explaining to him why they could never see each other again in the moving letter *De Profundis*.

In the film, Orlando plays a young rent boy who is the object of Wilde's attentions. The slightly androgynous, pretty-boy good looks he displayed as a teenager made him perfect for the role and, although he had just a single line to speak, there was an undeniable screen presence about the young man. Some actors have the ability to light up the screen; others don't. It was clear to anyone who saw *Wilde* that Orlando Bloom had celluloid charm. So, despite the fact that his was only a cameo role, *Wilde* was an important career moment: all of a sudden he found himself inundated with offers to appear in this film or to play that role. The temptation to grab any opportunity to work that came along must have been immense. Orlando did what few keen young actors would have done, and took what was, in hindsight, a very shrewd gamble: he turned them down.

Rather than jump in at the deep end without the training to back it up, Orlando took a more level-headed approach to his new-found exposure. He knew that if he didn't have the skill to take on what was being offered him, it could destroy his career before it had properly started. He had long

When Orlando moved to London, he found himself in with the party crowd.

had his sights trained on London's renowned Guildhall School of Music and Drama; his next step was to conclude his studies at this centre of excellence for young actors.

Clearly, you don't just walk into the Guildhall and expect to be given a place. The school's aim is to 'provide the highest attainable quality of education and professional training', and so competition for places is fierce. Aspiring students have to go through two rounds of auditions and interviews, and of the hundreds who apply every year, only a very select 24 are taken on to the three-year course. These then receive the benefit of an education at one of the profession's leading conservatoires, and have the opportunity to perform on one of the world's finest student stages in the 14 productions staged every year.

Needless to say, Orlando passed the auditions with flying colours.

Set in the somewhat unlovely environs of the Barbican Centre by the Thames, the Guildhall had, a few years earlier, seen stars such as Ewan McGregor (of *Trainspotting* and *Star Wars* fame) and Joseph Fiennes (*Shakespeare in Love*) walk through its hallowed portals. Orlando knew that if he played his cards right, he could match, or even exceed, their achievements. 'I always planned to go to drama school,' he explained

when looking back on his decision to attend the Guildhall. 'I suppose I could have trained in the industry more. But instead I chose an environment that was more conducive to experimenting.' Experiment he did. The list of the productions in which he performed at the school is nothing if not eclectic: *Little Me*, *Peer Gynt*, *Mephisto*, *Twelfth Night*, *The Trojan Women*, *The Seagull*, *Three Sisters*, *The*

From the first time the camera was pointed at Orlando, it was clear he had an undeniable screen presence.

Recruiting Officer, *Antigone*, *Uncle Vanya* and *A Night Out*. Orlando was spending time becoming the sort of actor who could perform Shakespeare, Chekhov and Ibsen with equal skill.

It was an essential period for him. He knew that he needed this rigorous classical training if he was to be at ease with the huge variety of complex roles he intended to perform later in his career. 'It was only when I went to the Guildhall that I started to feel like I got a proper education,' he explained when asked about his time there. 'We would learn about Milton and Donne and read Chekhov and Shakespeare and that kind of inspired me.' And, aside from studying the works of great writers, he was asked to do slightly more peculiar things: 'They encourage you to do all sorts of exercises to help you loosen up and be natural. You had to go and study animals at the zoo in order to find the animal's movements and whatever. I kind of wanted to be an ape, but my teacher insisted on me being a lizard so I wouldn't do things like beating on my chest. I had more stillness and composure. I was a lizard and that just meant that I had to hold this one position for hours on end and occasionally jog my head and stick my tongue out.' It certainly seemed that Orlando's acting education was covering all the bases.

'I was a lizard and that just meant that I had to hold this one position for hours on end and occasionally jog my head and stick my tongue out.'

ORLANDO BLOOM

Life was good. Everything was panning out the way Orlando had intended: he was working hard and playing hard and having a fabulous time. It was while he was at the Guildhall, however, at the age of 21, that he entered one of the darkest periods of his life.

It started out innocently enough: a quiet get-together at the flat of some friends. But the culmination of that evening would end up almost ruining not only Orlando's career, but also his life. The flat had a small roof terrace, but the door leading on to it had been warped by the weather and so could be opened only from the outside. Showing a certain bravado, Orlando decided that he should be the one to jump on to the terrace from the window and open the door. It was only a small jump, one that he could have managed easily. Instead, he decided to grab hold of a drainpipe outside the window before he jumped. That was his big mistake.

Unknown to Orlando or his friends, the pipe had rusted and was not even slightly secure. As he grabbed hold of it, it simply came away and he fell three floors on to another roof terrace below. It was only luck that stopped him from falling straight on to the railings that surrounded it. He couldn't walk; he couldn't even move his legs. In the hospital it became apparent that a normal X-ray was not going to enable the doctors to assess the extent of the damage to his spinal cord, so they conducted a scan and discovered that he had crushed one of his vertebrae, scratched a few others and bruised his spinal cord. In short, he was a mess.

When asked about those grim days in hospital, Orlando's answer is invariably the same. 'I nearly died,' he whispers. 'That accident took me to a very dark place I would rather not revisit.' The doctors told him they could try to operate – it was fortunate for him that he hadn't torn his spinal cord – but there was no way they could predict how successful the operation would be. There was a chance that he would never walk again; at the very least he was likely to be on his back for a minimum of six months, and he was forced to confront the possibility that he would spend the rest of his life in a wheelchair. And so, with Orlando fully aware of the possible outcome, the surgeons were called in.

His recovery was nothing short of miraculous.

Twelve days after the accident, and with the aid only of a pair of crutches, he walked out of the hospital. The surgeons were amazed, and although Orlando would need to put in a lot of gruelling physical work to regain his fitness – he couldn't remember how to walk at first, so he had to relearn that to start with – everyone who was involved with him at that time acknowledges that he had a very lucky escape. None more so than Orlando, who underwent

'I'm more **mellow** now than I was before ... An **accident** like that **really** does **change** you.'

ORLANDO BLOOM

a subtle but important character change as a result of that terrible accident. 'I'm more mellow now than I was before,' he explains. 'I approach things in a much more grounded, matter-of-fact, less flighty manner. An accident like that really does change you.'

If anything, his brush with death led to him becoming even more focused, and certainly more down-to-earth. They were attributes that were to serve him well in the months to come: Orlando Bloom's big break was just around the corner.

CHAPTER THREE

WACKO JACKO

'I WAS 22, I HAD TWO MORE DAYS
OF DRAMA SCHOOL AND IT WAS LIKE,
"HERE! HAVE A CAREER!" BOOM!'

ORLANDO BLOOM

While Orlando was busy completing his education, on the other side of the world a little-known director was formulating his plans for a movie that was to change the young actor's fortunes in a quite remarkable way. And not only was it going to be a career-maker for Orlando, it was also to become one of the monumental achievements of modern cinema. The director was Peter Jackson; the film, *The Lord of the Rings*.

The man who was to have perhaps the biggest influence on Orlando Bloom's career was born some 12,000 miles away in New Zealand on 31 October 1961. He was raised in Pukerua Bay, a small town west of Wellington, and, like Orlando, became obsessed by the cinema from an early age. When he was only seven years old he was given a Super 8 camera by his parents as a Christmas present; from that day on there was no looking back for the young Peter Jackson. He and his school friends started making their own films, and there was never any real doubt in the mind of the boy, or those who knew him, that movie-making was going to be the great love of his life.

In 1983 Jackson directed a ten-minute short film which he called *Roast of the Day*. He would spend the next four years developing this short into a full-length feature. He did this on a shoestring budget, pulling in favours from like-minded friends, and the result was the comedy schlocker *Bad Taste*. Sophisticated it was not: billed as an 'alien horror comedy', it was characterised by lashings of blood, guts, dismemberment and cannibalism. To the surprise of almost everyone, not least Peter Jackson, it became an overnight cult classic.

Jackson found himself in a situation not unlike the young Orlando Bloom after his big-screen debut in *Wilde*. All of a sudden he was being inundated with offers of work, and, more importantly, offers to move to the very hub of the film industry: Hollywood. Like

Peter Jackson: the man who made Orlando's dreams a reality.

Orlando, though, he decided that he would plough a more individual furrow. New Zealand was his home, the place he felt most comfortable and the place best suited to his own peculiar sense of self-expression. Just as Orlando had chosen to train in an environment more suited to experimentation, so Peter Jackson, unshackled by the restraints of Hollywood, could experiment with his very singular imagination. And so he resisted the temptation to move to Los Angeles, and elected to stay in the place he knew best.

The director followed *Bad Taste* with a film that was later to be described as '*The Muppet Show* on drugs'. *Meet the Feebles* was a curious mixture of puppets and comedy violence which consolidated Jackson's reputation as one of the quirkiest directors out there. His film-making continued in a similar vein until he surprised the industry and his growing fan base alike with the more intricate – and rather more humane – *Heavenly Creatures*. Starring Kate Winslet, it told the disturbing story of two schoolgirls who commit murder. *Heavenly Creatures* won Jackson and his partner (and co-screenwriter) Fran Walsh an Oscar nomination for Best Screenplay. It was a reminder to film buffs and industry players that Peter Jackson was a more multifaceted and complicated film-maker than his past work would suggest at

face value. He had an undeniable genius for taking the fantastical and the dreamlike and putting it up on screen. Despite his obvious talent, however, there were those who thought he was a strange choice to be trusted with the potentially financially disastrous project of shooting three ambitions films back to back. Could Peter Jackson really take on JRR Tolkien?

John Ronald Reuel Tolkien was born, like Harry Bloom, in South Africa. The son of a bank manager, he came into the world on 3 January 1892; when his father died his mother took him to England and they settled in Birmingham. Come the outbreak of war in 1914, he found himself conscripted and he witnessed first-hand the reality of battle and the camaraderie of men who fight together. After the war he pursued a career in academia, as a scholar and professor at Oxford of Anglo-Saxon, with a strong interest in Middle English and Chaucer. It saddened him that modern English literature did not have a piece of epic literature on the scale of *Beowulf* or *Sir Gawain and the Green Knight*. And so he set out to write one.

The Lord of the Rings, published in three parts in 1954–5, tells the story of Frodo Baggins, a hobbit of the Shire, who inherits from his uncle, Bilbo Baggins, a magic ring that renders anybody who wears it invisible, and grants to its owner unnaturally long life. The wizard Gandalf discovers that this is the ring forged by the evil lord Sauron in the fires of Mount Doom in faraway Mordor, and cut from his finger by Isildur and subsequently lost. It is utterly evil and must be destroyed. The only place the ring can be unmade is in the fires where it was first created, and so Frodo sets out on an epic journey to destroy the ring, accompanied by a fellowship of nine: Gandalf, Frodo's fellow hobbits Sam, Pippin and Merry, Isildur's heir Aragorn, Boromir of Gondor, Gimli the dwarf and the elf prince Legolas. When Boromir tries to steal the ring, the fellowship splits: Frodo and Sam make their way to Mordor alone, helped and hindered in equal measure by the revolting, tragic creature Gollum; Aragorn and the others prepare to do battle against the forces of evil.

Contemporary critics were divided as to the merits of Tolkien's magnum opus. Some compared him favourably with Milton, Spenser and Tolstoy. His publisher, Sir Stanley Unwin, suggested with some foresight that 'The Lord of the Rings is more likely to live beyond mine and my son's time than any other work I have printed.' The Sunday Times stated on the book's publication that the world would henceforth be divided into two groups of people: 'those who have read The Lord of the Rings, and those who are going to'.

> '*The Lord of the Rings* is more likely to live beyond mine and my son's time than any other work I have printed.'
>
> SIR STANLEY UNWIN, PUBLISHER

Others were less enthusiastic: it was described variously as 'a children's book which has somehow got out of hand' and 'dull, ill-written and whimsical'. It was criticised as being a fairy story, no more than a piece of escapism. But Tolkien could see no reason why there should not be an escape from the world of encroaching industrialisation. Like the hobbits, he was a lover of the natural world, and he felt he was witnessing the destruction of all that he loved by factories, machine guns and bombs. He always denied that there was anything allegorical about The Lord of the Rings, but the wicked deforestation of Middle-earth by Saruman is not a million miles away from what Tolkien feared for rural England.

No amount of poor criticism was enough to dampen the enthusiasm of his readers, however: the book became an instant best-seller and propelled Tolkien to worldwide fame, its popularity increasing as the years passed. In recent years, a number of surveys have been conducted to discover the favourite book of readers everywhere. *The Lord of the Rings* is invariably near the top.

Jackson had long been a fan of Tolkien's masterpiece. He was not the first film-maker to be attracted to the epic scope of the story. For years several scripts had been circulating in Hollywood, and an animated version had been made as far back as 1978. Because the film-makers ran out of money, the movie covers only about half of the book and an ambitious idea ended up as little more than a film buff's curio. But it is interesting to note that the part of Legolas, which would eventually be immortalised by Orlando Bloom, was voiced in this flawed early attempt by none other than *Star Wars*' C3PO, Anthony Daniels. There was even a rumour that the Beatles were planning their own adaptation of the book, with John Lennon playing Gollum, George Harrison as Gandalf, Paul McCartney as Frodo and Ringo Starr as Sam. Unsurprisingly, Tolkien himself put the kibosh on that one.

It came to be received wisdom that *The Lord of the Rings* was unfilmable. And yet the history of this remarkable book is one of overcoming the seemingly impossible. After all, Tolkien himself had achieved the astounding feat of creating an epic that rivalled Homer and Chaucer in the sheer

JRR Tolkien – the man Orlando says created a world without limits.

scope of its vision and yet remained accessible to modern readers of all ages. Was nobody up to the task of repeating this achievement on celluloid? It's true, however, that in terms of the nuts and bolts of movie-making, the book had nothing in its favour. For a start, it was too long: surely no studio would commit to filming each part of the trilogy with little or no guarantee that it would actually work. Moreover, the book's very scope was too vast to be faithfully recreated on the big screen.

And yet the narrative sweep of *The Lord of the Rings* had captured the imagination of several film-makers. It's not hard to see why, as the themes with which it deals are classic motifs of great drama: good and evil, loss and friendship, unrequited love, the nature of kingship. As a young man Peter Jackson immediately recognised its filmic potential: 'I first read the book when I was 18. I thought at that time that it would make a great movie and I was looking forward to seeing it one day. I never dreamed in a million years that it would be me doing it.' The years passed, and nobody took up the challenge of putting the ambitious novel on the screen. Suddenly Jackson realised that technology had moved on to such an extent that it was perhaps now possible to do Tolkien's work justice on the big screen. And still no one rose to the challenge.

Jackson's motto has always been that he makes the films that he likes to see personally. If no one else was going to shoot *The Lord of the Rings*, he had better do so himself.

With screenwriters Fran Walsh and Philippa Boyens, he worked on a two-movie adaptation of the book. He was astonished when executives at New Line cinema suggested that they should shoot it as three movies. He had been presented with an enormous opportunity, but with that came a responsibility to get it exactly right.

Jackson instinctively understood that there was no way he could translate the book line for line to the screen. The secret of adapting such a huge work was to lie in the director's ability to capture the spirit of the original, to be

'I think Tolkien created a world where there were no limits and I think Peter Jackson captured the essence of that in the way that he directed the films.'

ORLANDO BLOOM

faithful to Tolkien's vision even if the restraints of the medium meant he could not be entirely truthful to his narrative. 'I started with one goal,' explained Jackson. 'To take movie-goers into the fantastical world of Middle-earth in a way that is believable and powerful. I wanted to take all the great moments from the book and use modern technology to give audiences nights at the movies unlike anything they've experienced before.'

Orlando himself expressed Jackson's genius quite concisely: 'I think Tolkien created a world where there were no limits and I think Peter Jackson captured the essence of that in the way that he directed the films.'

Jackson would soon prove that, more than any other contemporary director, he was the one best suited to adapt *The Lord of the Rings*. Before he got anywhere near a camera, he was going to have to make important decisions. The most difficult were those choices that would have the most direct effect on the films' success in the eyes of the world's countless Tolkien enthusiasts: location – he needed to make sure that his sets really looked like Middle-earth in all its astonishingly rich variety; and, of course, casting – the actors he employed had to be able to portray the characters the fans knew so well with great flair and accuracy.

The director's location problems were solved almost before they started. He was a New Zealander; New Zealand was where he had always lived, and where he intended to continue working. Fortuitously for him, the two islands that form this small country contain within their compact area some of the most diverse and magnificent scenery in the world. Within the confines of New Zealand, Jackson managed to find locations for the rural idyll of Hobbiton, the giddy magnificence of the Misty Mountains, the parched wasteland of Mordor and the medieval splendour of Minas Tirith.

If the issue of location was relatively easily solved, the problem of casting was to prove a little more difficult.

It is to the credit of the makers of *The Lord of the Rings* that, in terms of casting, they managed so successfully what could easily have gone badly wrong. In fact, their achievement is such that images of the characters in the movies have to a great extent supplanted the images that previously existed in the minds of Tolkien fans everywhere. This is no mean feat. If Gandalf, for example, had not been just so, the film would have failed. Happily, Ian McKellen proved to be an inspired choice for the role: in *The Fellowship of the Ring* he captured the slightly grumpy, slightly disorganised Gandalf the Grey, an immortal wizard with very human weaknesses; in *The Two Towers* and *The Return of the King* he perfectly makes the transformation into the more determined, more spectacular Gandalf the White.

All the other actors achieve a similar level

27

of performance: Christopher Lee as the baleful, malevolent Saruman; Viggo Mortensen as the noble, heroic Aragorn; Bernard Hill as the feudal Shakespearian King Theoden; Sean Astin as the stalwart, loyal Sam. The list goes on and on, and nowhere do the film-makers miss the mark. But one character stands out as being perhaps the most complicated to capture on the big screen. That character is Legolas the elf.

The difficulty of casting Legolas can be understood by looking at Tolkien's description of the elves of Middle-earth. For one thing, they are immortal, unless killed by force. Unlike humans, they do not decline physically as they age, but grow wiser and more beautiful. Because of their great age and great wisdom they also carry the burden of great sorrow, accumulated through the long years of their lives. And, while they are fair and peace-loving, they can also be fearsome creatures: their skill with the bow and arrow, their sharp hearing and superhuman eyesight make them accomplished warriors, and their history is filled with the tales of great battles.

Legolas himself is the son of Thranduil, king of the elves of Northern Mirkwood. In Tolkien's complicated elven dialects, his name derives from the words *laeg* (green) and *golas*

The mismatched – and sometimes hilarious – pairing of Legolas the elf and Gimli the dwarf.

(collection of leaves). For this reason he is often referred to as Legolas Greenleaf. Tolkien does not specify his exact age, but from clues in the book it can be estimated as being around 2,780. Nor does he describe Legolas's features at any length, though he does say that he is 'fair of face beyond the measure of men'. He does, however, describe the elf's father as having long golden hair, and it is not unreasonable to assume that the son has inherited this. Legolas's eyes are bright, his hands long and slender; he treads so nimbly that his feet hardly create any footprints in the snow. He can run for miles without getting exhausted and he can shoot an arrow with more precision than anyone else in Middle-earth.

'Fair of face beyond the measure of men.'

TOLKIEN ON LEGOLAS

Fair of face beyond the measure of men; 2,778 years old; long golden hair; nimble yet fierce. How on earth was Peter Jackson going to capture all of these attributes in one person?

It was one of the most difficult hurdles the film-making team had to negotiate in the pre-production stages of the films. Jackson

29

remembers it well. 'We were getting worried because we hadn't seen anyone who'd be right for the part. The character had to be graceful, elegant and poised, all the qualities elves should have.'

Enter Orlando Bloom.

Back in London, Orlando was coming to the end of his three-year course at the Guildhall School of Music and Drama. He had a few successful jobs under his belt, but his decision to complete his acting training meant that he had not had the exposure he might otherwise have gained. If any time was ripe for him to be offered a major film role, this was it; when his agent called to tell him that a group of New Zealand film-makers were preparing to shoot *The Lord of the Rings* on the other side of the world and would he be interested, Orlando's excitement was palpable.

Strangely enough, he was initially asked to audition for the part of Faramir. Faramir is the son of Denethor, the steward of Gondor, and was ultimately played memorably by David Wenham. It's easy to see why Orlando was a prime choice for the part: young, good-looking, heroic, Faramir displays on screen all the characteristics of earnestness and suaveness that would have suited Orlando down to the ground. In fact, Jackson had decided to offer Orlando the

part and just hadn't told him yet, when he suddenly had a brainwave: why not ask the young English actor to fill the boots of the character that was giving him so many headaches – Legolas Greenleaf?

Orlando was invited to audition for the role, and he remembers it as if it were yesterday. 'I thought, Definitely! Game on! So I learned the scene and acted it on videotape.' Clearly what he did in that short audition pressed the right buttons with Peter Jackson. Suddenly everything fell into place for the director: the fellowship was complete.

'Shortly after,' remembers Orlando, 'I got this incredible phone call saying they were offering me the role. It was like winning the Lottery. Like having all your dreams fulfilled. It was amazing!' We can only imagine what must have gone through his head the moment he took that life-changing call. But Orlando had turned down roles before. Was that something he planned to do this time round? Evidently not. 'I was 22, I had two more days of drama school and it was like, "Here! Have a career!" Boom!'

It was a dream come true. How could Orlando not have been the envy of his fellow students at the Guildhall: not yet out of college, he had landed a leading role in what promised to be the biggest movie of all time. Would this young guy's luck never fail!

CHAPTER FOUR

RESPECT YOUR ELF

'THEY ARE THE FIRST-BORN, THE OLDEST AND
THE WISEST OF THE RACES IN MIDDLE-EARTH.
THEY ARE AGELESS AND IMMORTAL.'

And so it was that the 22-year-old, fresh out of drama school, found himself on a plane to New Zealand, the country that was to be his home for the next two years. They were to be years of considerable development for Orlando. He had learned his craft in theory; now he was going to have to put it into practice – a prospect at once exciting and daunting. On top of that, the move must have been quite a culture shock for the young man: he was being plucked from his life as a carefree clubber in the heart of London – perhaps the most exciting capital city in the world – to find himself on the other side of the planet, 12,000 miles from his family and friends.

In his bag was a copy of *The Lord of the Rings*. He had read it once to prepare for his auditions; now, however, he was going to have to study it in much greater depth. He had been given the chance to immortalise Legolas Greenleaf on the big screen and, if he got it wrong, the fans would never forgive him. He couldn't just rely on his make-up to transform him into the immortal elf: it was going to take more than a pair of pointed ears and a long, blonde wig to create a convincing screen persona. Orlando would have to get under the skin of the character if he was going to have any chance of making the role work. (The ears helped, of course. Were they

uncomfortable? 'Not at all, other than the two hours it took to put them on. I went home one night without the wig but with the ears on, crawled into bed with my girlfriend at the time, and woke up with one ear stuck to my pillow and the other still there…')

There can be little doubt that from the start Orlando had an intuitive understanding of the job in hand. 'They are the first-born,' he explained when describing how he approached the project, 'the oldest and the wisest of the races in Middle-earth. They are ageless and immortal. They have never known sickness or pestilence. They can be slain in battle or die of a broken heart – but otherwise that's about it. Tolkien's elves are nothing like the traditional image of pixies and fairies: they have great physical and mental strength and are powerful, full-blooded people.

'As for Legolas, he has seen the world. He is incredibly experienced in many ways. I thought it was essential to get the physicality right. Elves are immortal and have a superhuman strength; but they are graceful and elegant like cats. You know how cats can jump and land steady on their paws? That's how I tried to be. It's very balletic.'

The way Legolas moves is how Orlando found his way into the character. How would the elf walk? How would he run? 'Cat-like' describes perfectly the impression Orlando achieves in the movie. He is fast and lithe; constantly aware, he does not blink; he is the very incarnation of stealth and subtlety; he is reserved, and never speaks unless he has to; but he is always poised and ready for action.

'You know how cats can jump and land steady on their paws? That's how I tried to be. It's very balletic.'

ORLANDO BLOOM

Legolas is a great warrior, so Orlando set out to combine this almost feline reserve with the focus of someone who is fully adept at the martial arts – he even went so far as to describe his character as a 'Zen elf'. He can pick up any weapon and use it without difficulty. He is the kind of elf you want on your side in a fight.

But there is more to the role than this. Throughout the film every character develops, and Legolas is no exception. Orlando immediately saw this as well. When we first meet him in *The Fellowship of the Ring*, he has an aloofness borne of being part of a race who would not ordinarily deign to interact with other species such as humans – and particularly dwarves, whom elves see as dirty little creatures who steal from the earth without putting anything back. But as the fellowship continues on its journey, and the bonds of friendship are strengthened, Legolas seems to ease into his relationship with this mismatched group, and even learns a sense of humour. In fact, the growing fondness and banter between the elf and Gimli the dwarf give rise to some of the trilogy's most enjoyable moments.

Orlando was the first of the cast to arrive in New Zealand. As the all-out action elf, he was going to have to learn a whole batch of new skills, and so the first two months after his arrival kept him extremely busy. 'The first thing they did,' he recalls, 'was put a bow in my hand.' As Legolas, he was going to have to learn how to wield a bow and arrow convincingly – that is the character's weapon of choice, and he would have to look completely expert when he handled it. Archery is a difficult discipline – perhaps the most difficult that any of the cast would have to learn. Orlando spent his first week studying hard, and by the end of that week was able to shoot paper plates out of the sky – not bad for someone who had never handled a bow before.

Elves would never saddle a horse, so the next skill on Orlando's list was to ride bareback. This is no mean feat, but gradually he became an accomplished horseman, and

33

by the end of his training he had ridden about 20 different horses. His riding lessons did not prevent the occasional mishap, though: on one occasion Orlando cracked a rib when he fell off his horse. Fortunately it wasn't an injury serious enough to affect filming, but it was enough to make some of Legolas's more spectacular moves uncomfortable, to say the least.

Skill with a bow and arrow wasn't the only weapons training he was going to need. Legolas is also an adept swordsman, so Orlando would have to be one too. In the film, the elvish manner of fighting is based on ancient European and Asian martial arts. A special sword-fighting trainer was employed to teach the young actor how to use his sword convincingly.

Orlando drew his influence for Legolas from Akira Kurosawa's *The Seven Samurai.*

But Orlando's pre-filming lessons were not limited to the physical. Tolkien's work is fully realised in every way, and one important aspect was the language of the elves. This did not exist in the real world, of course, and so Tolkien, an expert in archaic tongues, created it. Orlando, along with others in the movie, had to learn a new language if he was going to appear convincing. Tolkien in fact invented a number of languages; the one that is most frequently used in *The Lord of the Rings* is that of the Sindarin elves. It was formulated by the author to have a linguistic character very like Welsh, as he felt that the story itself was closely related to Celtic mythology. When Orlando, Viggo Mortensen or Liv Tyler speak in elvish in the film, it is not just gobbledegook. It is a fully realised, intricate and accurate language – and one that Orlando had to come to grips with before he even set foot on the set.

Orlando also dug deep into the archives of film history. One of his principal inspirations for the Zen-like character of Legolas was the 1954 film *The Seven Samurai* by Japanese director Akira Kurosawa. This tells the tale of a village under attack from bandits which is defended by the samurai, whose reserve and focus enable them to outwit – and outfight – their enemy. It was through studying the movements and actions of the samurai warriors that Orlando learned

to take on Legolas's aura of focus and quiet determination.

Orlando knew that *The Lord of the Rings* would be a make-or-break job for him, and he knew that it would be a very big film indeed. But even he was not quite prepared for the vastness of the production, and it wasn't until he first arrived in New Zealand that it was brought home to him. 'One of the first things I did,' he explains, 'was visit the special effects studio and there was a warehouse full of armour and thousands of rows of weapons.

'One of the **first** things I did was visit the **special effects** studio and there was a **warehouse** full of **armour** and **thousands** of rows of **weapons**. That was the first time I thought, "**God**, this is **going** to be **huge**."'

ORLANDO BLOOM

That was the first time I thought, "God, this is going to be huge."'

And huge it was. Director Peter Jackson had embarked on this project with a gusto bordering on obsession. Like Orlando, he knew that this was to be a turning point in his career: he had to get it right, and that process had started well before Orlando, or any other actor for that matter, arrived in New Zealand.

Jackson's main concern in the early days of pre-production of the movie was authenticity. Hobbit holes, elvish realms, dark towers: they all had to not only appear real but also correspond with the mental picture so many fans have had of these places over the years. One of the director's first moves was to employ the two most experienced artistic interpreters of Tolkien's world alive today – Alan Lee and John Howe. As illustrators of previous editions of the book, Lee and Howe had produced fabulous renditions of the locations of *The Lord of the Rings*, and Jackson wanted them on board from day one.

His brief was at once straightforward yet daunting: 'He said he wanted to be as true to the spirit of the books as he could, and try to create very, very real landscapes and as believable a world as possible,' explained Alan Lee. Once engaged, he and Howe produced literally hundreds of sketches which formed the basis of the production design of the movies. Sketches became storyboards, storyboards became models and sets, and the illustrators' vision was realised in the minutest detail.

With Lee and Howe on board, Jackson started gathering around him a group of the most talented designers and artists in the world. Early on in the development of the film, he decided – ambitiously – that every single prop would be made from scratch. And so the artisans set about creating over 900 suits of armour, over 2,000 replica weapons, over 20,000 everyday objects and over 1,600 pairs of prosthetic ears and feet. All of these were made with an almost fanatical attention to detail – even the safety weapons made of rubber were practically indistinguishable from the real thing. Over 200 gruesome prosthetic orc heads were made – individual masks, each one with its own personal characteristics. A special goo, not unlike tar, was even created to represent orc blood.

Hobbiton is wonderfully recreated and enchants all who see it: the dark Mines of Moria are breathtaking and terrifying; Saruman's tower is eye-popping in its immensity; and the magnificent re-creation of the statues of the Argonath create one of the most impressive visual moments in the history of cinema.

But it was perhaps on the creation of the elves and their habitats that the most attention was lavished. The homes of Orlando's kinsmen needed to be both utterly magical and quite real. When the elegant Legolas first appears on screen, it is in the elvish city of Rivendell, and it is immediately clear that his quiet mysticism is perfectly matched by his surroundings. Rivendell is above all peaceful, a place of contemplation. The successful portrayal of its serenity is no accident – every last corner is designed down to the last detail, from the gurgling stream that flows through the centre of the town, to the hand-carved statues and door frames. In the background, individually crafted 40-foot towers shimmer inscrutably, telling us there is more to the place than meets the eye.

Similarly the magical kingdom of Lothlorien was created by building 100 individual elvish houses; the film-makers even went to the lengths of attaching more than 2,000 fake leaves to the trees to give the impression of foliage.

The devil, as Peter Jackson realised very early on in the project, would be in the detail, and he knew that the detail would have to be worked on from day one. It was into this environment of almost fanatical creativity that Orlando Bloom arrived to don the bow and cloak of Legolas Greenleaf.

Orlando's learning curve was to be steep. Not only was he being thrust into this hotbed of unprecedented, spectacular movie-making activity, he was also going to have to share the screen with some of the finest actors in the world. He was really going to have to pull out all the stops if he did not want to be utterly upstaged by actors of the calibre and experience of Ian McKellen and Christopher Lee.

Sir Ian McKellen is recognised throughout the world as one of the leading actors of his generation. His skill as a Shakespearian actor is second to none, and the sheer versatility of his performances has won him more than 40 significant acting awards in a career which has spanned more than four decades. Christopher

'Vig [Mortensen] used to call me "elf boy" and I called him "filthy human". He was always saying how prissy elves are, and I always answered, "Well, at least I'm going to live forever. Did you hear me? Live forever!"'

ORLANDO BLOOM

Lee is no less than a legend. Born in 1922, he is one of the most prolific and experienced actors of all time, having appeared in more than 250 film and TV productions; indeed, he is listed in the *Guinness Book of Movie Facts and Feats* as being the international star with the most screen credits. Perhaps best known for his spooky performances in a host of Hammer horror movies, he has worked with

Hollywood legends as diverse as Orson Welles, Steven Spielberg and Tim Burton.

Orlando was anything but blasé about working with such luminaries of the film world. 'When I was at drama school,' he admits, 'Ian was someone we all looked up to. I've got to work with some of the best in the business. They all go about their craft in their own way. It's been really interesting to observe that. I've learned a lot from watching the people around me.' Like a sponge, Orlando went about the process of absorbing all the artistic influences that came his way, but the one actor who had more influence than any other on him was less well known than McKellen, Lee, Ian Holm or any of the other big names: Viggo Mortensen.

'Viggo was like a mentor for me,' admits Orlando, 'without anything being spoken. I used to sit next to him on the make-up bus, and find myself just staring at him while he was having his make-up done and drawing in his book or writing his notes. I would find myself fascinated.' And not without reason, for Mortensen is one of the most fascinating men in the world of film. Born in New York to a Danish father and American mother, he spent much of his early life travelling: he lived in America, Venezuela, Argentina and Denmark. He made his screen debut in 1985 playing alongside Harrison Ford in Peter Weir's

Viggo Mortensen influenced Orlando more than anyone else on the set of *The Lord of the Rings*.

Witness. Before *The Lord of the Rings*, worldwide fame had eluded him, but his many performances were invariably praised by both audiences and critics. Film is only one aspect of his artistic endeavours, however: he is a keen poet and an accomplished photographer – a true modern-day aesthete.

More than anything, it was Viggo's unassuming dedication to his work that affected Orlando. 'He really influenced the way I approach the work today. He has a lot of integrity in terms of how he approaches it, but he can also have fun with it as well, so it was cool. He taught me a lot.'

Orlando and Viggo also injected a welcome note of light-heartedness into the relentlessly hard-working atmosphere of the shoot. 'Vig used to call me "elf boy" and I called him "filthy human". As an elf, I never got dirty, and Vig was always covered in blood and sweat. He was always saying how prissy elves are, and I always answered, "Well, at least I'm going to live forever. Did you hear me? Live forever!"'

If Viggo took the role of mentor, the rest of the cast – especially the hobbits – became firm friends. It's perhaps only to be expected that spending so much time together over such an extended period would result in a special kind of friendship, but according to Orlando it went that little bit deeper. The most important thing for him that he took away from his time in New Zealand was 'the fellowship in terms of the friendships that we made, the connection we made with each other. You don't make friends like that easily. These are people who I will love and be friends with for life.'

Friendship has its ups and its downs of course and, when a group of people work so closely together, tempers inevitably become frayed. Dominic Monaghan, who plays Merry the hobbit, recalls one such moment. 'Orlando and I got into a real fight. My triceps were really painful from working out, and one night he came up behind me and pinched my arm. I said, "Don't do that!" and he did it again. That was it.' What followed was genuine fisticuffs – Monaghan tactfully refrains from revealing whether the hobbit or the elf came out best in the tussle; yet it says much about the strength of the relationships formed during that epic shoot that even full-blown fights were not enough to sour the friendships that endure to this day.

Dominic and Orlando made up, and they are still the best of friends, as are all of the fellowship. 'I was just back in LA,' Orlando revealed recently, 'and I went surfing with Billy [Boyd] and Dom a few times. I saw Elijah [Wood], and we all went out for dinner one night. And I saw Sean Astin at some awards ceremony. Whenever we get together, it's as if nothing's changed.'

The bond between the nine members of the fellowship was so close that each of them – with the exception of John Rhys-Davis, who plays Gimli the dwarf – had a tattoo of the elvish figure for '9'. (Rhys-Davis sent his stunt double in his stead.) It was not Orlando's first tattoo – he has had a sun on his stomach since he was 15 – and, as he quite pertinently points out, having a tattoo is not to be undertaken lightly. It's with you for life.

A bit like a movie.

Orlando remains friends with Dominic Monaghan – despite the occasional bout of fisticuffs.

CHAPTER FIVE

MAKING
HISTORY

'THESE GUYS ARE THE BRAVEST MEN IN THE WORLD.'

A young, fit, good-looking actor prepares himself in a Wellington studio for a spectacular stunt. Previously his character has been calm, collected, mystical; but now it's time for a fight. And not just any old fight – Legolas the elf is going to have to floor a cave troll. A short, bearded director with scraggly hair and a pair of shorts instructs him to jump up on to the beast's shoulders and fire arrows into its head. There's just one small problem – there's no beast. The actor is fighting an imaginary foe, and it is testing all his thespian skills. He's giving it everything he's got. 'Pete,' he shouts at the director, 'you'd better make this a really gnarly beast! This better be one nasty bastard, otherwise I'm going to feel a complete fool!'

Later the young star looks into the distance. 'The eye of the enemy is moving,' he whispers. He turns, his face a study in fear. 'He is here.'

'Cut!' shouts the director.

The actor smiles. 'Pete,' he says. 'You'd better make that one *bad*-looking eye!'

Orlando Bloom wasn't the only person who had to put all his trust in director Peter Jackson. Studio executives, distributors, money men – but perhaps the actors most of all. It was to be them up on the screen, them who would look foolish if it didn't all turn out as it should have. And it can't have been easy, especially on a film that relied so heavily on special effects. So many of the characters and locations were to be 'painted in' afterwards that it was the ultimate test of their skills – and their faith in the guy in charge. Orlando put it succinctly: 'You had to completely put all your heart, trust and faith into Pete and just know that he was going to pull it off.'

> 'So I had my bow up, but the horses weren't going to stop. Gimli fell – he landed on top of me – and I landed on a rock. I cracked a rib, and Vig cracked his tooth.'
>
> ORLANDO BLOOM

Put their faith in him they did, even to the point that they put their own well-being at risk. 'We were doing this scene with 30 horses lined up,' Orlando recalled later. 'We had to shoot it five times. We had to ride over this mound and down into a gully, and then there were rocks and a sheer drop. Well, horses are pack animals and, when that many horses get going, they're really going. On the last take, the director said, "Now, imagine the orcs coming up from behind." So I had my bow up, but the horses just weren't going to stop. Gimli fell – he landed on top of me – and I landed on a rock. I cracked a rib, and Vig cracked his tooth.'

That was just one of the hairy situations in which these actors found themselves. This was action film-making; a laid-back Merchant Ivory production it was not. On another occasion, when the cast and crew were filming the spectacular scene of the fellowship passing the huge statues of the Argonath in their boats, Orlando found himself in a canoe with Gimli's stunt double, Brett. Suddenly it became apparent that the water was flowing too quickly; if they weren't careful, the actors were going to find themselves in the dangerous waters downstream. One of the crew jumped in to the rescue and grabbed the end of the canoe to stop it travelling any further. But the current was too strong and, as he held the boat firmly in place, water started flowing over the sides: the boat was sinking. 'Let go of the boat, man!' cried Orlando, but it was impossible to know what to do for the best, and suddenly the safety boats were rushing in.

Brett, who was wearing heavy chain-mail armour, was sinking fast. Quick as a flash, Orlando grabbed him and yanked him up out of the water, holding on to him to stop him going under again before the safety boats could come to the rescue. Peter Jackson later mused that 'Orlando was more embarrassed than anything, to be the one member of the fellowship who sunk his boat while on active duty.' Maybe he was; but it seems more likely that he was relieved to have been able to save Brett as he did.

The adrenalin was not just flowing on the set. In fact, Orlando went out of his way to look for it; and for an adrenalin junkie like Mr Bloom, New Zealand is the place. A quick glance at the young man's medical history might make you think he would be going out of his way to avoid putting himself into positions of potential danger: apart from his broken back, and the unfortunate incident with the horse that led to him breaking his ribs, Orlando has broken his nose, both legs, a wrist, an assortment of fingers and toes – oh, and he has cracked his skull three times too. You might suppose a list like that would make him think he'd got all the action-boy antics out of his system. Think again.

The film's producer, Barry Osbourne, made a point of writing to the young actors as soon as they arrived telling them that on no account were they to take part in any of the extreme sports for which New Zealand is famed. It was like a red rag to a bull. 'The first thing I did in Queenstown was to go to do a bungee,' Orlando admitted later. He stood on the platform for an hour before plucking up

'I like to confront my fears. If something really terrifies me, I'll just jump into it so it doesn't terrify me any more.

the courage to take the plunge, but that kind of daredevil stunt is right up his street. And his penchant for jumping from great heights was not just restricted to bungee jumping: he threw himself out of an aircraft in a sky-diving extravaganza that would have had his producer's heart skipping a beat if he'd known about it. Add to that the snowboarding and surfing with which he filled his time when he wasn't on set, and you have an idea of the lengths to which Orlando would go to get his adrenalin fix.

But there is more to his love of these extreme sports than simply a desire to get the blood rushing. It tells us a lot about what it is that makes him tick as an actor. 'I did it because I wanted to challenge myself, face my fears and prove a point to myself. I don't suffer from any serious phobias like vertigo, but even so it's still pretty terrifying when you are standing on the edge of a bridge about to throw yourself off into a huge ravine with just a piece of rubber band tied to your legs. I like to confront my fears. If something really terrifies me, I'll just jump into it so it doesn't terrify me any more. That's why I got into acting. I went to stage and drama school because I used to get really freaked out standing on stage.' So in the Orlando Bloom view of the world, doing a bungee jump or jumping out of a plane is not so unlike taking on the challenge of a massive film project like *The Lord of the Rings*: even though doubts and insecurities might be nagging at your brain, the most productive response is to throw yourself with gusto into whatever it is that scares you. Only then can you be the master of your fears.

It's not a bad outlook for a young actor with superstardom in his sights.

'I did it because I wanted to challenge myself, face my fears and prove a point to myself.'

ORLANDO BLOOM

Of course, Orlando's thrill-seeking activities were restrained by safety harnesses and crash helmets. The chances of him coming to any harm at all were very low indeed. The same could not be said of a group of young soldiers who, when Orlando was only 16, were sent on a mission where their safety was anything but guaranteed. Their exploits were to form the basis for his next film.

In 1993 the Arab state of Somalia was in a position of turmoil. Ravaged by a civil war that was ripping it apart, the country was also in the throes of a famine of almost biblical proportions. The combination of these two factors had led to the death of more than

47

300,000 people. As if this were not enough, Somalia was in the hands of a tyrannical warlord by the name of General Mohammed Farah Aidid. As food aid came flooding in from richer countries, Aidid was effectively stealing it: the food intended for the starving never reached them; instead it went to line the pockets of this most unscrupulous of politicians. The United Nations were trying to establish a coalition government formed from Aidid's opponents, but were encountering violent opposition from the warlord.

General Mohammed Farah Aidid – the dictator who sparked the events of *Black Hawk Down*.

The United States decided that something had to be done. It would be too difficult to target Aidid – he would be guarded by the most impenetrable security – so they decided on the next best thing. If they could remove the general's top men, they would weaken his power and maybe, just maybe, restore order.

It was a mission fraught with danger. A hundred and twenty crack American troops were to enter the city in Black Hawk helicopters, abduct the carefully targeted officers and return to base. It was supposed to take about an hour; the reality was very different. Two of the state-of-the-art helicopters were shot down. Their occupants found themselves stranded in the hostile city of Mogadishu, under fire from all directions. One helicopter was captured and held in a secret location by an angry mob. All day and all night the Americans fought for their lives and, by the time they were rescued, 18 were dead and 73 were wounded. The inhabitants of Mogadishu fared rather worse: it is estimated that 500 Somalis lost their lives in those bloody few hours. And while the mission was a success in strictly military terms – the two targets, Omar Salad and Mohammed Hassan Awale, were caught – in every other respect it was one of the most cataclysmic events the American military had ever had to cope with.

The story of the Battle of Mogadishu is one

of well-laid plans gone very wrong, of terrible mishaps and astonishing soldiering, of tragedy and heroism, of bravery and of cowardice. In short, it was the stuff of movies, and it was no surprise when Hollywood decided to immortalise it on celluloid. The man for the job was the important and versatile British director Ridley Scott. In the years to come he was to make a profound impact on the career of Orlando Bloom.

Born in the north of England in 1937, Ridley Scott started his career as a commercials director, but once he had graduated on to feature films it didn't take long for him to make his mark. In 1979 he released the classic horror movie *Alien*, which put his name firmly on the map. He went on to direct such influential films as *Blade Runner* and *Thelma & Louise*, and had perhaps his finest hour so far with the magisterial epic *Gladiator*.

Scott is known for taking pride in his ability to spot, encourage and nurture young talent. He gave Sigourney Weaver her big break in *Alien*; the young Harrison Ford was offered the lead role in *Blade Runner*; and Russell Crowe only became the international superstar he is today after his appearance in *Gladiator*. When it came to the job of casting for the movie that was to become *Black Hawk Down* he characteristically chose a mixture of established artists – including Josh Hartnett

and former Guildhall student Ewan McGregor – and unknowns, like Orlando Bloom.

By the time Orlando got the call offering him a part in *Black Hawk Down*, *The Lord of the Rings* was in the can. There would be reshoots and ADR – the process of re-recording the voices – but the bottom line was he needed a job. *The Fellowship of the Ring* was yet to be released; his name was yet to be in lights. It was another stroke of luck in the career of Orlando Bloom that he caught the attention of a director who has built up a reputation for helping actors hit the big time; when Scott was looking for someone to play the part of Private Todd Blackburn, a young soldier eager to fight heroically for his country, Orlando fitted the bill perfectly.

Todd Blackburn is the youngest of all the soldiers involved in the Mogadishu mission; he is also its first casualty. He falls from a helicopter and – ironically, given Orlando's own history – breaks his back. The soldiers have a code of conduct: don't leave a fellow soldier when he's down, so his comrades do all they can to help him.

Like Peter Jackson, Ridley Scott was a stickler for detail when it came to designing and filming *Black Hawk Down*. There is, however, one big difference: *The Lord of the Rings* is set in a fantastical world, a world of the imagination; the events of *Black Hawk*

Down were all too real and, even if the movie took a somewhat partisan look at the battle, the cast and crew knew they had to go out of their way to ensure they accurately captured the atmosphere of those terrible few hours if the film was going to hit the mark. Orlando was used to this kind of desperately accurate film-making, and once more his training started long before the cameras began to roll.

The cast were sent off to boot camp to get a taste of the military lifestyle. As producer Jerry Bruckheimer later said, 'We felt that it was really important for the actors to actually become part of the military, even for a short

'We wanted **actors** to have **respect** for the **military** and understand the **physical challenges** that they go through.'

JERRY BRUCKHEIMER, PRODUCER

time, if they were going to portray soldiers. We wanted actors to have respect for the military and understand the physical challenges that they go through. If you talk to any soldier who has been through a battle or a war, they'll tell you that the only thing that saved their lives was either the man next to them, or their training.'

The actors were given classes which ranged from general military knowledge – how to wear the uniform, how to address fellow soldiers and officers – through to marksmanship and hand-to-hand combat. They learned how to tie knots, and how to use radios. They practised firing M16-A2 rifles and automatic weapons. They were instructed in the importance of teamwork and attention to the most minute details of a combat situation.

Jason Isaacs, one of Orlando's co-stars, summed up the most important piece of knowledge the actors took away with them. 'We thought that it was an unwritten rule among the Rangers that you don't ever leave a man behind but, when we got to Fort Benning for training, we learned that it's a *written* rule. The Ranger creed is recited every morning, *en masse*, wherever they are. And they mean every word of it, because, in a conversation with the Rangers who were in Mogadishu, every single one of them said that their first instinct, after learning about the crashed Black Hawks, was to get out there to the site and bring back every single one of their brothers. It is a bit of a culture shock for us actors to understand their philosophy. The Rangers were fighting for the guy on their left, and the guy on their right.'

Once the actors' groundwork had been

'When you see helicopters
and guns going off, there
really were helicopters and
guns going off. There wasn't
a lot of acting going on.'

done, it was over to the film-makers. Ridley Scott recreated a battle environment that was shocking in its realism. Jason Isaacs describes the actors' experiences on set: 'The first time we had to do any shooting, Ridley said to me, "Right, you're coming along the street, you're going to walk down and all this shit is going to break loose. The whole building's going to come down, cars will blow up and all these people will be shooting, and just get to the end and do your lines." So I come down the street and everything just blew up like mad – it was like a World War.'

Orlando described it more succinctly. 'When you see helicopters and guns going off, there really were helicopters and guns going off. There wasn't a lot of acting going on.' The result was a harrowing movie

> ## 'They are heroes, they were all undoubtedly heroes.'
>
> ### ORLANDO BLOOM ON THE BLACK HAWK SOLDIERS

experience. Ridley Scott avoids becoming too political in his representation of the battle, deciding instead to focus on the reality of war and the personal involvement of the soldiers fighting it. Watch *Black Hawk Down* and you almost feel as if you are fighting the battle yourself. 'They are heroes,' explains Orlando,

'they were all undoubtedly heroes. There were some decisions that were made further up the chain that didn't help … but these guys are the bravest men in the world.'

By the end of 2001, when Orlando was only 24, he was preparing for the release of two major movies. When *Black Hawk Down* hit cinema screens, it won plaudits from critics and audiences around the world. But his part in that film, though crucial and significant, was not a large one, and it was not going to make his name. That role was left to *The Fellowship of the Ring*.

When the first instalment of *The Lord of the Rings* trilogy was released worldwide in December 2001, audiences were agog. It is no overstatement to say that they had never seen the like of this film before, and scarcely a person came away without being aware that they had just seen movie history in the making. Even the usually jaded and cynical critics waxed lyrical, and superlatives abounded: it was a masterpiece of cinematography; it took film-making to new heights; it set a standard which films in the future would find difficult to match; it married a fabulous narrative, breathtaking special effects and a depth of characterisation that few critics were expecting, or thought they would see the like of ever again.

And in the middle of it was Orlando Bloom.

CHAPTER SIX

ROBIN HOOD
DOWN UNDER

'HE SPOKE TO ME ABOUT SHOOTING
GUNS AND RIDING HORSES IN AUSTRALIA.
IT SOUNDED FANTASTIC…'

There were a number of critics who, instantly they saw *The Fellowship of the Ring*, drew parallels with another ground-breaking trilogy which had been released 25 years earlier. Although the *Star Wars* movies had little in common with *The Lord of the Rings* in terms of narrative, they were nevertheless comparable in terms of the effect they had on the viewing public; a whole generation of young cinema-goers were to be weaned on Peter Jackson's epic in the same way that their parents' cinematic experiences were practically defined by *Star Wars*. And yet what of *Star Wars*' leading actor? Mark Hamill was doomed to a life of obscurity, whereas his foil Harrison Ford went on to be one of the most successful leading men in Hollywood's history.

For the hitherto unknown actors in *The Lord of the Rings*, it was a cautionary tale. They understood only too well the risks of being typecast, and they knew that, despite the unprecedented success of the movie, their careers were in the balance, to be tipped on either side by the choices they made next. Twenty years hence, would they be consigned to daytime television shows asking 'Where are they now?', like Luke Skywalker; or would their careers go into intergalactic hyperdrive, like Han Solo? For the more established actors, it wasn't likely to be a problem: Ian McKellen and Christopher Lee had already ploughed a successful furrow. But Orlando and the hobbits knew they were on the brink of unbelievable success or the gloomy mediocrity of a lifetime of attending *The Lord of the Rings* fan conventions. The next two movies that Orlando filmed showed that he intended to make his work as diverse as possible: there was no way he was going to get stuck in a rut.

'It was so rewarding playing a character who was a hero in real life to so many Australians. It was gratifying to discover the historical details, to explore the impact of the Kelly gang and to know the effect those men had on the entire nation. It really moved me.'

ORLANDO BLOOM

If *The Lord of the Rings* successfully created a modern mythology, the story of Ned Kelly belongs firmly in the realm of modern legend. He might not have been instantly familiar to children and adults in Britain and America, but in Australia he is a household name. He has become a southern-hemisphere Robin Hood, a figure whose story has changed in the telling but who remains a colourful, heroic part of Australia's history.

The tale of the outlaw Ned Kelly and his gang has become a tale of heroism and a struggle against a corrupt system. Whether that is a true representation of the Kelly gang's exploits is open to discussion. To some, Kelly was a murdering outlaw, a scoundrel who deserved to be hanged; to others he was a noble hero fighting single-handedly against injustice on behalf of those too weak to do it themselves. But most Australian schoolchildren today will tell you that, like Robin Hood and his band of Merry Men, they were figures to be admired.

Ned Kelly was the son of a convict who had been deported from Ireland to Australia for stealing a sheep; he grew up amid a culture of convicts, many of whom had been driven to their crimes by the terrible circumstances in which they found themselves – and in Australia those circumstances were scarcely any better. While still in his teens, Kelly was imprisoned for a crime he did not commit – stealing a horse – and remained behind bars for three long years. When he was released, he discovered that a corrupt policeman was making unwelcome advances to his sister. His friends, including the charming ladies' man

The Kelly Gang Armour.

Joe Byrne, saw the suitor off, but the policeman exaggerated the story and claimed that Kelly had attempted to shoot him. Kelly, Byrne and the gang were outlawed; when they were discovered by two policeman, Kelly shot them in a kill-or-be-killed situation. A record price was put on their heads and the public were told they could be shot on sight with impunity. The outlaws' close friends were imprisoned in an attempt to get them to reveal their whereabouts. Kelly's mother was sentenced to three years' hard labour.

Railing against the injustice of their situation, the Kelly gang started robbing banks; they used the proceeds in part to help the families of those who were being oppressed by the corrupt authorities. They soon became national heroes, symbols of a potential uprising that the government felt they had to repress at any cost.

The story of the Kelly gang has intrigued and inspired film-makers and writers since the time the events took place at the end of the 19th century. It was even the basis for what is believed to have been the world's first feature film: *The Story of the Kelly Gang* (1906). In those early days of cinematography, when the Americans were only making short films which could fit on a single reel, the Australians were developing a thriving movie business. This was before the days of sound, but they didn't need talkies to start a huge following. It was somewhat slapdash film-making – a far cry from the exertions of the likes of Peter Jackson and Ridley Scott a century later – but it didn't need to be anything else: this was new and exciting.

The most popular subject for those early movies was the exploits of the bushrangers – outlaws in the Australian bush. One of the most important directors of the day was Raymond Longford, who described the process of making these films: 'They would take their gear down to the bush at Brookvale, outside Manly, camp out for a week, and without any script make a film. Their action was usually a stagecoach hold-up, a lot of galloping and a shooting match.' It was a crude formula, but an effective one.

After *The Story of the Kelly Gang* enjoyed great success, other outlaws, such as Captain Starlight and Captain Thunderbolt, were chosen as subjects ripe for the picking. Bushranger films became so popular that the New South Wales Police banned them in 1912, saying they encouraged bad behaviour. It left a gap in the market that was soon filled by an American equivalent: the Western.

The Story of Ned Kelly toured Australia for nine years. Today only fragments of the original survive, amounting to just a few minutes of footage – some of which was found by chance in a rubbish dump in Melbourne, slung out by its unsuspecting owner. Over the years, though, the story was to catch the eye of more than one creative talent. In 1960 a TV version of the story was made, and Mick Jagger starred in the 1970 film *Ned Kelly*. In 2001 the Booker Prize was won by Peter Carey's novel, *True History of the Kelly Gang*. In the spring of 2002 it was the turn of director Gregor Jordan to immortalise the story once more on film.

> 'He spoke to me about shooting guns and riding horses in Australia.'
>
> ORLANDO BLOOM ON *NED KELLY* DIRECTOR GREGOR JORDAN

Orlando Bloom was in Los Angeles when he met up with Gregor Jordan to discuss his latest venture. 'He spoke to me about shooting guns and riding horses in Australia,' recalls Orlando. 'It sounded fantastic, but I have to admit I didn't know a lot about the real-life Ned Kelly or the members of his gang.' That didn't matter to the director. He had already cast the abrasively good-looking Heath Ledger in the title role; now he was looking for the perfect actor to play Ned's sidekick, the boyish, charming womaniser Joe Byrne. At the time Byrne was seen as being by far the most glamorous member of the Kelly gang. His trademark was his high-heeled boots, and he was handsome and rebellious in equal measure – enough to set any young lady's heart fluttering. With his model features and smouldering good looks, Orlando Bloom fitted the bill perfectly.

He clearly relished the prospect of playing the part. As he was doing the publicity rounds for *The Fellowship of the Ring* he constantly referred to a 'top-secret' project down in Australia. And perhaps more than in *Black Hawk Down*, he was being offered an opportunity to play a role that he could really sink his teeth into. 'It was so rewarding playing a character who was a hero in real life to so many Australians. It was gratifying to discover the historical details, to explore the impact of the Kelly gang and to know the effect those men had on the entire nation. It really moved me.' It also offered him the opportunity to return to his Antipodean way of life. 'I just loved working in Australia, I really enjoyed the pace of life. It's got so much to offer, it really has.'

Maybe it was the script, maybe it was the surroundings – maybe it was just the fact that he didn't have to have a long, blonde wig or a shaved head ('It was great to work with my own hair,' he later chuckled) – but, whatever it was, something certainly clicked for Orlando in the making of *Ned Kelly*. The reviews were not universally good, and certainly the movie came nowhere near *The Lord of the Rings* or *Black Hawk Down*, but there were few who disagreed that Orlando was the shining star of the film. He caught with perfection the

57

irrepressible and inimitable charisma of Joe Byrne that made him such a lady-killer; that talent for characterisation that his drama teacher had noticed so many years before was truly maturing and bearing fruit. He showed a thorough understanding of the role he was to play. Of Byrne he says, 'He was a very different man from Ned Kelly. He was quiet, more thoughtful, and Ned often relied on him for advice. He was definitely his right-hand man. Sure, he smoked opium, but he was generally much more reserved than the other members of the gang. The first time he was arrested it was for the possession of meat. Can you imagine that?'

In addition to his natural talent, Orlando once more drew inspiration from being in the hands of a director who implicitly knew the fine details of his subject. Gregor Jordan spoke convincingly of the conflict at the heart of the legend of Ned Kelly. 'We were a penal colony, so there was this great criminal subculture with a very much working-class ethos, and this very strong cynicism towards authority, which I think is still extremely prevalent in Australia. To me, Ned Kelly just embodies that spirit down to the ground. Someone who's fighting against corrupt oppressors, and doing it with a twinkle in his eye. That's the spirit that Australians really identify with – well, a lot of Australians anyway.

'Mind you, the Kelly story does divide the community. There's a lot of people in the legal fraternity and even the police force who think that Ned Kelly was just a thug and a criminal and deserved everything he got. A lot of other people don't see him that way. They see him as a hero.'

Orlando perfectly caught the twinkle in the eye of which Jordan spoke – and his Irish accent wasn't so bad either. Off set, he took great delight in practising that lilting brogue, to the extent that he would use it when out and about in bars and restaurants. And he didn't just limit it to his time filming *Ned Kelly*. 'I love that Irish accent,' he revealed. 'Sometimes I'll even use it in LA when I go out with friends. It's good for a laugh.'

With the filming of *Ned Kelly* complete, Orlando had another successful role under his belt – and had made another good friend. He had become close to Heath Ledger during the making of the film, and it was a friendship that he would continue to value over the next few years, even if they had no plans to make another movie together in the foreseeable future. He was particularly pleased to watch a real-life romance bloom between Ledger and the film's love interest, Naomi Watts. The sexual chemistry that existed on screen between the two was clearly not just a matter of clever acting.

Orlando, Heath
Ledger and the rest
of the Kelly Gang.

Orlando perfectly caught the twinkle in the eye of the womanising Joe Byrne.

Another friendship Orlando made on *Ned Kelly* was to have a very profound effect on his already blossoming career. Geoffrey Rush was not really given the opportunity to excel in his role as the policeman on the trail of the outlaw gang, but he had more than proved his credentials in previous outings. A veteran of blockbusters such as *Shakespeare in Love* and *Elizabeth*, he is one of the most engaging Australian character actors of his generation. Rush's next project was to be a fun-filled, swashbuckling Disney romp in which he would play the twisted captain of a cursed ship, and he couldn't help thinking that there might just be a part in it for young Orlando Bloom. The role was that of an eager young artisan by the name of Will Turner. The movie was called *Pirates of the Caribbean*.

Pirates of the Caribbean was to be the movie that would turn Orlando Bloom from a fairly well-known actor into a global superstar, but it nearly didn't happen. Orlando was attached to a very low-budget British project that was a far cry from the extravagant multimillion-dollar films that he had been used to working on. To some it might have seemed an odd choice – after all, why not stick where the big money and the worldwide exposure is? But it says a great deal about his integrity as an actor that he decided to follow *Ned Kelly* with this small, independent movie. It says even more that he was prepared to turn down starring alongside Johnny Depp because he had already given his word that he would star in *The Calcium Kid*.

On the plus side, this was to be Orlando's first leading role. The fact that it was not going to be massively high-profile was perhaps an advantage. The pressure of carrying an expensive film on the back of your skills as a leading man is a considerable one. By taking the title role in a small movie Orlando was being characteristically shrewd: he was learning the ropes once more, getting a feel for the responsibility of taking on a role which could make a project live or die.

The Calcium Kid is a light-hearted, tongue-in-cheek comedy. Orlando plays Jimmy, an ordinary, run-of-the-mill milkman who suddenly finds himself in an extraordinary position. Through a series of bizarre events (and helped by the fact that his bones are good and strong from drinking plenty of milk – hence the Calcium Kid) Jimmy finds himself in the position of fighting the world boxing championship in his home town. It's a quirky concept – about as far as can be imagined from the gritty realism of *Black Hawk Down* or *Ned Kelly* – but Orlando certainly enjoyed doing it. 'I love doing big epics like *The Lord Of The Rings*,' he says, 'but it's great to play a character who's less cool. This milkman is just an everyday geezer, a bit naive, who's suddenly thrown into the public eye. I can relate to that.'

The film's director, Alex de Rakoff, a first-timer who also wrote the script, had put together a cast of largely unknown British actors. There were a few stars there who could be described as being household names (pop singer Billie Piper plays Jimmy's love interest with a charming assurance), but the director understood the importance of having a name like Orlando attached to his project. It could make or break the movie, and so he was keen to give the actor free reign to interpret the part however he wanted to. 'Orlando was an interesting choice for me,' he revealed,

63

'I love doing **big epics** like *The Lord of the Rings*, but it's great to **play** a character who's less cool. This **milkman** is just an **everyday** geezer, a bit **naive**, who's suddenly **thrown** into the **limelight**. I can relate to that.'

ORLANDO BLOOM

'and he actually changed my complete opinion of how this character should play out. We're very lucky to have got him and he's done a really wonderful job.'

Orlando spoke of his director in similarly elevated terms. 'He's such a strong actor's director in every sense of the word. He just knows how to get the right performance out of you and he's been a lot of fun to work with.' But he did admit that the finished film was very different to how he had imagined the project would look, although he didn't seem to think that that was necessarily a bad thing. 'It wasn't what I thought it was going to be, but I really liked it. This is much more a kind of teenie sweet comedy. But it's good. I think it will be liked. There's nothing not to like about it. It's cool.'

He understood that the risk of a movie not quite turning out the way you expect is all part and parcel of the process of film-making, and of learning the ropes as an actor. 'That sometimes happens – not always – but I suppose it's part of the job, isn't it? At the end of the day you have to put yourself in the hands of the people who share your vision – or you share their vision. But essentially there's kind of a rite of passage as a young actor and you have to pay your dues. Fortunately I've been able to do that in great movies. I'm hoping that now … soon anyway … I can start doing stories that I really want to do and work with directors that really want to work with me.'

It would be two years before *The Calcium Kid* was released. In fact, its cinematic release was limited to the UK. In America, where a small British film like this would get lost, it was scheduled to go straight to video. Orlando, though, had bigger fish to fry. He was leaving the rainy streets of London, where *The Calcium Kid* had been shot, to head for sunnier climes. Despite his insistence that he had to fulfil his previous obligation to Alex de Rakoff, the schedules had somehow righted themselves: Orlando was flying out to play the role of Will Turner opposite an actor who knew a thing or two about being a heartthrob. His name was Johnny Depp.

CHAPTER SEVEN

A PIRATE'S
LIFE FOR
ME

'I DON'T STAB AS MANY STUNTMEN AS I USED TO.'

Forty thousand feet above sea level, two impossibly handsome men – one in his 20s, one in his 40s – are sharing a drink or two. Both have delicate cheekbones, piercing eyes and a boyish pout. Not far away, one of the most powerful men in Hollywood is sitting with his wife. Jerry Bruckheimer looks on as Johnny Depp and Orlando Bloom get acquainted, and drunk. On board this private jet, which Johnny has chartered to take his co-star and his producer from Los Angeles to St Vincent in the Caribbean, millions of dollars' worth of Hollywood talent are having a very jolly time indeed. Away from the enquiring gaze of fans and eager celebrity-spotters, these beautiful, rich and influential people can really let their hair down. It's the only way to travel.

'Jerry was up at the front of the plane with his wife,' remembers Orlando, 'and me and Johnny and Johnny's friend Sam were at the back of the plane and we sat there and drank red wine. I don't know, maybe the altitude had something to do with it, but when we got to the island we just crawled off the plane staggering.' It must have been quite a sight: as the plane taxied round Joshua airport, a red carpet was unfurled for the stars to meet the prime minister of St Vincent, who awaited Orlando and Johnny with his full entourage.

As the doors to the plane open, the welcoming committee is astonished by the vision of Johnny Depp, roaringly drunk, singing and dancing down to the tarmac. His young protégé, Orlando Bloom, bent double with laughter, follows behind him, picking up the bits and bobs that Johnny has dropped in his wake. Depp arrives at where the prime minister is standing, stops, smiles – then gives him a big hug and a kiss.

> 'Johnny's been a sort of guideline for me as a young actor, and for probably anyone of my generation.'
>
> ORLANDO BLOOM ON JOHNNY DEPP

The pirates had arrived in the Caribbean.

Even movie stars have heroes, and Johnny Depp had always been one of Orlando's. 'Johnny's been a sort of guideline for me as a young actor, and for probably anyone of my generation.' Orlando's desire to ensure that his career is defined by interesting movie choices derives in part from his admiration of Depp, whose filmography is nothing if not eclectic.

Born in Kentucky in 1963, Johnny Depp was the son of an engineer and a waitress, and went off the rails before he was even a teenager. In those wild years of his life he

Master and apprentice –
Captain Jack Sparrow and
Will Turner.

gave little thought to the possibility of being an actor; music was in his blood, and like so many before him he embarked on the stony path of trying to make it as a rock 'n' roll star. At 16 he dropped out of high school, and soon found himself playing underage in bars with a punk outfit called the Kids. The Kids achieved some success, supporting such big-name acts as Talking Heads, the B-52s and Iggy Pop; but by the age of 20, married to make-up artist Lori Anne Allison, Depp found himself struggling for money – at one point he was reduced to taking a job selling ballpoint pens over the phone. It became apparent that he was going to have to find some other way to make a living; with good looks and charm like his, Lori surmised, why on earth should her husband not try acting?

And so she introduced Johnny to Nicolas Cage, a friend of hers. Cage in turn insisted that Johnny meet his agent: the net result was a part in Wes Craven's *A Nightmare on Elm Street*. Depp saw it as a one-off – music was still his life and he hoped that the Kids were going places. They didn't. Soon they split, and Johnny found himself accepting a part in a sub-standard teen comedy called *Private Resort*. It was not one of cinema's proudest moments, but he was beginning to develop a taste for being on the big screen. He decided that, if he was going to do it, he would do it

properly, and enrolled at a drama school. The result was a part in Oliver Stone's Oscar-winning Vietnam movie *Platoon*, but after that it rather went downhill.

Depp starred in a number of TV movies and series before reluctantly accepting a role in a new police drama, *21 Jump Street*. It was an immediate and massive success. Johnny Depp became a household name, a teen idol, and rich. But he was unsatisfied. This was not the kind of work he saw himself doing. He felt stifled by his own success, and when *21 Jump Street* came to an end he was determined to make his next career choice interesting, different and kooky. He found the perfect vehicle in Tim Burton's *Edward Scissorhands*. The story of the terribly scarred, razor-fingered orphan, it was a million miles from *21 Jump Street*. It could have gone horribly wrong, but Johnny had two things on his side: he was in the hands of one of the most skilful, imaginative directors working today; and his own undeniable skill as an inspired character actor was allowed to shine through. It turned out to be the best career move he could have made.

A string of weird and wonderful films followed: *Benny and Joon*, *Arizona Dreaming*, *Ed Wood*, *Fear and Loathing in Las Vegas*, *Sleepy Hollow*, *From Hell*. With each one Johnny's worldwide audience grew bigger and bigger, and his fans knew that whenever they saw him on screen they would never run the risk of being presented with something humdrum. His desire, after *21 Jump Street*, not to rely on his good looks meant he made choices which few other actors would have dared to make, and turned down roles others would have grabbed eagerly – the lead role in *Speed*, for example, which eventually made a star out of Keanu Reeves, or Tom Cruise's part in *Interview with the Vampire*. Depp declined the obvious and relished the curious; he took every part and turned it creatively and ingeniously into his own.

Crucially, though, he never lost a sense of the absurdity of it all and, despite being desperately serious about the work, never started to take *himself* too seriously: he was more than happy to lampoon himself in the British comedy series *The Fast Show*, and his less-than-sophisticated on-set humour is well known throughout the business.

Johnny Depp was absent from screens for a while, thanks to his involvement in Terry Gilliam's ill-fated *The Man Who Killed Don Quixote*, which collapsed mid-filming. When he reappeared, even his most hardened admirers thought that perhaps he had lost the plot. He had accepted the lead role in a Disney movie based on, of all things, a ride in a theme park. It was an unfortunate provenance, and

even the most generous observers predicted that it could be a less-than-successful movie-making venture.

But out of tiny acorns, great oak trees grow. If the tiny acorn in this instance was a 15-minute theme-park ride, it was watered and nurtured by Hollywood's most precious substance: talent. Jerry Bruckheimer had long harboured an ambition to make a pirate movie. 'I loved watching pirate pictures as a kid,' he explained when asked about his decision to produce *Pirates of the Caribbean*. '*Treasure Island*, *Captain Blood* and *The Black Pirate* were some of my favourites. Errol Flynn and Douglas Fairbanks were formidable and, although their movies are still exciting and very watchable today, I thought we could add some extra pizzazz to a popular theme.'

'I loved watching **pirate** pictures as a kid … I **thought** we could add some **extra pizzazz** to a **popular** theme.'

JERRY BRUCKHEIMER, *PIRATES OF THE CARIBBEAN* PRODUCER

No film is anything without a good script, and so Jerry Bruckheimer employed the skills of Tinseltown's finest. Ted Elliott and Terry Rossio had been nominated for Academy

Awards and were involved with the blockbusting animated film *Shrek*. From the slightly shaky premise, they constructed an intricate, elegant story that combined the swashbuckling antics of Errol Flynn with a darker, supernatural thread. Captain Jack Sparrow was once captain of the notorious pirate ship the *Black Pearl*, until his first mate, the deliciously wicked Captain Barbossa, led a mutiny against him. The mutineers then steal some Aztec gold which places them under an unholy curse that turns them into skeleton-type ghosts, doomed to exist in a state between life and death until every piece of the gold is recovered and returned. The last piece of gold is in the possession of the beautiful Elizabeth Swann. When she is kidnapped, the poor blacksmith Will Turner rescues the unscrupulous pirate Jack Sparrow from the gallows, and enlists his help to find her. What follows is one of the most entertaining, action-packed, sinister and funny pirate tales ever to grace the silver screen.

So much for the narrative. The next thing on Bruckheimer's shopping list was a director who could bring together the disparate strands of this complicated story. Gore Verbinski had recently scored a very palpable hit with the utterly terrifying remake of the Japanese horror movie *The Ring*. Now he was being brought on board to deliver a ghost story with a difference. The success of *Pirates of the Caribbean* would lie in the ability of Verbinski to deliver two movies at once: a tongue-in-cheek ghost yarn and a thrilling adventure story that would be popular with children and adults alike.

But the glue that would hold the whole film together was always going to be the actors, and the most important decision Bruckheimer had to make was who was going to play the three lead roles of Will Turner, Jack Sparrow and Captain Barbossa.

Jerry Bruckheimer had discussed the role of Will Turner with Orlando Bloom when the two were involved in the filming of *Black Hawk Down*. 'When we first cast him, I knew his time would come,' recalls the producer. 'I just didn't know how lucky we'd be to grab him before all the frenzy started with the two *Lord of the Rings* films. I actually talked to him about this role while we were on *Black Hawk*, and he thought it sounded like a wonderful character.' But time passed, and there were other films to be made; the idea of Orlando in this role was clearly a good one, though. Geoffrey Rush had suggested to him that he audition for the part when the two of them were filming *Ned Kelly*. 'Geoffrey Rush was very excited about coming over for *Pirates*,' recalls Orlando. 'He told me about it and said, "There's a great role that you've just

Geoffrey Rush – the deliciously wicked Captain Barbossa – knew that Orlando would make a perfect Will Turner.

got to read, if nothing else."' Then *The Calcium Kid* got in the way; unwilling to let anyone down, he honoured his commitment to that film. When it finally transpired that Orlando would be able to make *Pirates of the Caribbean* after all, it seemed as if everything was coming together to ensure that he filled the boots of Will Turner.

So once more Orlando found himself on

'I was already familiar with the way Jerry does business – it's very slick, very tight and he does his best to cover every detail and make sure everything is done the right way.'

ORLANDO BLOOM ON
JERRY BRUCKHEIMER

the set of a major production, surrounded by the finest talent in the world, and in the hands yet again of film-makers who went about what they were doing with vigour, enthusiasm and attention to detail. 'I was already familiar with the way Jerry does business – it's very slick, very tight and he does his best to cover every detail and make sure everything is done the right way. You see the same work ethic in everyone at his company; it's amazing and it's

a trait that gives an actor security. This project just had all the right elements.'

The shoot was not without its mishaps, however. Early on, a fire in the Disney studios caused $350,000 of damage to sets for the movie. Buildings were evacuated, firemen were called in. Amazingly, nobody was hurt, but it took a considerable effort to get the schedule back on track after that almost disastrous setback.

Pirates of the Caribbean was a real test of Orlando's acting mettle. Sharing the screen with performers of the stature of Johnny Depp and Geoffrey Rush would be one of the biggest challenges he had faced so far. Certainly he had appeared in major films before, but this was his most prominent role; if his ability wasn't up to it, it would be thrown into sharp relief against the skills of some of the finest actors working today. And although it may not have seemed like the most demanding role available to the young actor, as with so many things the skill lay in making a difficult job seem easy. Johnny Depp himself encapsulated the intricacies of Orlando's task, and had nothing but praise for the way in which he went about it. 'Orlando was amazing. He probably had the most difficult role in the film because he plays the straight, earnest, upright character who, in a lot of ways, is the eyes and ears of the audience. I thought he pulled it off beautifully.'

The role of the straight man is one of the most difficult to play successfully, especially opposite a show-stopping performance like Johnny Depp's. Depp relished the idea of creating an idiosyncratic pirate from the moment the script dropped through his letterbox. 'It was a different kind of role for me. It was a great opportunity to invent this pirate from the ground up, to create a different kind of pirate than you have seen before.' And was there more to it than a desire to satisfy his muse? Of course. 'Isn't it every boy's dream to be a pirate and get away with basically anything? Who wouldn't want to play a pirate?' Who indeed? But there are few people who could manage it with the skill, flair and downright gumption of Johnny Depp.

Orlando remembers being amazed when he first realised what Depp was doing in front of the camera. 'I was so envious of the character that he created. I mean, that character was not on the page, it wasn't written like that. That's what Johnny does, he creates an incredible character from something that's an idea on a page.

'When I read the script, Jack Sparrow was a great swashbuckling pirate that you could see Errol Flynn doing something with. I've seen Johnny's movies, I've seen what he does to a character. But I don't really think the studio thought he was going to do what he did. He created this kind of drunken, sea-legged, Keith Richards sort of number. With the costume, the gold teeth, the eye make-up, the whole thing, he sort of "Depped" it.'

Depp himself acknowledged the debt his characterisation of Jack Sparrow owed Rolling

'Keith has always been a great hero to me and I felt that pirates of the 18th century were sort of rock'n'roll stars. Who better than Keith Richards to be your inspiration?'

JOHNNY DEPP ON THE ORIGINS OF CAPTAIN JACK SPARROW

Stone Keith Richards. 'Keith has always been a great hero to me and I felt that pirates of the 18th century were sort of rock'n'roll stars. Who better than Keith Richards to be your inspiration?'

Together, Orlando and Johnny worked fiendishly hard to achieve the result they wanted. Both actors found the spectacular sword-fighting scenes the most difficult to master. Orlando had had some experience with swords from filming *The Lord of the Rings*, which he found helpful ('I don't stab as many stuntmen as I used to,' he joked), but it still took a long time to master. The result, as seen in the first extended fight between Will Turner and Jack Sparrow, was spectacular. 'It was a headache to make,' Orlando admitted, 'and kind of intimidating. But it was a lot of fun to film as well. Once you learn the moves, it's like muscle memory. You can then play with it and have fun with the scene.' And fun is certainly what they had.

From that first drunken plane ride through to the final day of shooting, Orlando absorbed the influence of Johnny Depp like a sponge. 'He's somebody who, as a young actor, and most young actors I think would probably agree, you grow up seeing this guy who's probably one of the best-looking guys on screen, but he just manages to become these incredible characters and really morph into that.' Not only did he learn a great deal about the craft of appearing in front of a camera – he certainly did that – he also took away a great deal in terms of Depp's approach to his work, and to the life of a movie star in general.

'I kept thinking, man, I'm sharing the screen with Johnny Depp. How did that happen? It's amazing to work with somebody you admire and for them to surpass your expectations. It was interesting to observe how he goes about his craft. He's so grounded. I just picked his brains about how he goes about living his life, because it must be an unusual reality. I just wanted to know how he deals with that. He was so gracious, and such a lovely man. He far surpassed all my expectations, just as a human being, let alone as an actor. It was just so reassuring.'

Depp undeniably offered the younger actor some invaluable advice that would set him in good stead if his career followed the same trajectory as it had over the past couple of years. 'This is a great job,' he told Orlando, 'and we all really enjoy doing it. It's not open-heart surgery. Enjoy the whole process. You keep certain things private, don't you? There are things in your life where there is a line … *this* I'm prepared to talk about.' Johnny certainly understood a thing or two about people wanting to know more about his life than he necessarily wanted to let on. Since his divorce from his first wife, Lori, he had been linked with a series of beautiful women, such as Winona Ryder and Kate Moss, before finally settling down with French pop singer Vanessa Paradis. The net result was a remarkable interest in his life from the world's media, an interest that led him to

The *Pirates of the Caribbean* team. (Left to right) Gore Verbinski, Jack Davenport, Orlando, Keira Knightly, Johnny Depp and Jerry Bruckheimer.

become almost reclusive with his family on an estate in the south of France. 'The one thing I can tell you,' he warned when Orlando commented on the ridiculous amounts of money that were being spent on this big-budget movie, 'is that privacy and security become really expensive.'

'You're going to **take** a few **bullets**, a few **snaps** taken here and there. You can't **avoid** it, but you **can** avoid fuelling the **fire**.'

ORLANDO BLOOM ON FAME

It wouldn't be long before Orlando began to experience a taste of what Johnny Depp had had to learn to live with. His previous movies had been big, and he had certainly established a global fan base for himself; but the release of *Pirates of the Caribbean* would send his sex-symbol image into the stratosphere. Literally hundreds of fan websites sprang up; teenage girls declared undying love for their hero 'Orly'; he was on the front cover of magazines all around the world; any list of the world's top-ten sexiest guys featured Orlando somewhere near the top. Suddenly he became one of the world's most eligible young men; he began to feel the glare of the world's media on him,

interested in every last detail about not just his working life, but also his personal life. Now the advice of his mentors such as Viggo Mortensen and Johnny Depp became very relevant indeed.

Amid the mayhem and the frenzy, Orlando remained level-headed and philosophical about it all. 'The truth is, I understand people wanting to know about your private life in some way, because they want to feel like they are getting closer to you. But you have areas where you don't want to go. You're going to take a few bullets, a few snaps taken here and there. You can't avoid it, but you can avoid fuelling the fire.'

As speculation about Orlando's personal life grew – he was linked to beautiful women, sometimes accurately, sometimes not – he became more and more reluctant to talk about it publicly. He was beginning to understand that, although he was achieving what he always wanted, there was a flip side to fame. The secret was learning how to manage it. 'That's the hard thing when you start to live the dream. It's not quite what you thought it was, because there is a lot of stuff that comes on top of it, and you kind of have to figure it all out.'

But if he thought things were big now, even he cannot have been prepared for the exposure that was just over the horizon.

CHAPTER EIGHT

TROY BOY

'I WAS OUT WITH BRAD IN MALTA. WE WALKED
OUT OF THE LITTLE TAVERN WHERE WE HAD
SOME DRINKS AND FLASHBULBS EXPLODED. HE
WAS SWAMPED. HE STARTED A SMALL RIOT.'

In the thick of the most spectacular battle scene ever to grace the big screen, an elf with long, blonde hair has a look of steely determination on his face. He has just slaughtered countless orcs and he's up for slaughtering a few more. Around him all is chaos, and yet he maintains his Zen-like calm. He performs his most spectacular stunt so far, using a shield to surf down a flight of steps, all the time firing a flurry of arrows which, as always, hit their countless marks. The audience cheers.

On another cinema screen somewhere else, the charismatic, eager young Will Turner has realised that it's OK to bend the rules a little bit – well, quite a lot – as he rescues the beleaguered Jack Sparrow from the noose in a swashbuckling sequence that is keeping everyone on the edge of their seats. Swords flash, more stunts are performed – and again the audience cheers.

Throughout 2003 there was a lot of cheering for Orlando Bloom.

The Two Towers had been as big a hit as everyone had expected. More spectacular than *The Fellowship of the Ring* in every way, the second part of the trilogy wowed audiences across the globe. Crucially – and for some unexpectedly – it allowed the characters to develop and evolve; for many, one of the high points of the story was the continuing relationship between Legolas and Gimli, a source of much of the film's humour. It's a tribute to Orlando's acting technique that he managed to combine Legolas's aura of focus with a cheeky glint that added richness and life to the movie.

Legolas was fast becoming one of the trilogy's most popular characters. Audiences loved his spectacular action sequences – most noticeably the scene in which he leaps on the back of a cave troll in *The Fellowship of the Ring*, and the shield surfing in *The Two Towers* – and so director Peter Jackson decided to give Orlando the opportunity to go out with a bang in the final movie and give him his most astonishing few moments of screen time yet. 'He loved the way the audience responded to that stuff, those moments,' Orlando said. 'And so he wanted to top it. That's all Pete, man – that boyish lust for life. He's got such a great appetite for it all and he just wanted it to be bigger and better.'

The scene is during the Battle of the Pelennor Fields. The stronghold city of Minas Tirith is under attack from all sides and from all manner of creatures – including the enormous, monstrous elephant-type animals Tolkien named the Mumakil. Jackson's idea was to have Legolas fell one of these creatures – and the wild men riding it – single-handedly, and so he flew Orlando back out to New

Zealand for the re-shoots. It was a typically intricate operation. 'I basically spent three days on, like, three thousand sandbags that had been piled up creatively to make the ass-end of an elephant, and then they add a rig on top with the stunt guy so I get to fight on top of him. I was swinging around on wires and climbing up the arrows – and then I had a very serious conversation with my digital double to make sure he knew exactly what his motivation was.'

'I was swinging around on wires and climbing up the arrows – and then I had a very serious conversation with my digital double to make sure he knew exactly what his motivation was.'

ORLANDO BLOOM

The result was awesome – one of the most spectacular moments of a spectacular movie. When *The Return of the King* was unleashed on a public eager with anticipation, it exceeded their already high expectations, just as Orlando always knew it would. After all, he explained to anyone who asked, the final third of a movie is always the most exciting, and *The Return of the King* was the final third of the most ambitious and, according to some, the finest movie ever made.

That final trip to New Zealand was tinged with sadness for Orlando. He had spent nearly two years of his life there, and nearly four years on *The Lord of the Rings*. Now it was all coming to a close. As the principal characters finished their final re-shoots, they were each given a memento from the movies. Orlando was presented with his bow and arrow, and the clapperboard from his last scene. He didn't leave New Zealand without a lump in his throat. 'It's very sad to say goodbye to such a great character like that,' he admitted at the time. 'I was really connected to Leggie for such a long time. It was kind of a coming-of-age time for me being in New Zealand, but it's nice to have the sense that it has come to a natural close.'

No matter how high his star rose in the future, he would never forget he owed his success, to a large extent, to a pointy-eared elf in a story about furry-footed hobbits, and to the director who made it into the cinematic event of a generation.

Pirates of the Caribbean had lost Orlando his anonymity. Beforehand, even with the kind of exposure he gained from *The Lord of the Rings*, he could walk down the street without attracting too much attention. Now those

days were past, and he was going to have to get used to the fact that his face was known – and admired – throughout the world. There were down sides to this, of course, but they were far outweighed by the up sides, one of the best being the fact that he could now take his pick of some of the most exciting roles on offer.

The success of *The Lord of the Rings* had awakened Hollywood to the fact that epic stories were big business. It was hardly surprising then when it was announced that a big-budget adaptation of the most famous epic in all of history was about to go into production: *The Iliad* by Homer. And it was just as little a surprise when the casting directors came knocking on Orlando Bloom's door.

The Trojan War is perhaps the most enduring story in Greek history, part fact and part mythology and best known through Homer's epic account *The Iliad*. Phrases such as 'Trojan horse' and 'Achilles heel' have become commonplace in our modern language, and even those who do not quite know the entire story at least have some idea of what it is about.

Paris was the youngest son of King Priam of the ancient city of Troy. At his birth, it was foretold that he would lead to the downfall of Troy; in order to counter the prophecy he was

The smouldering Paris.

sent from the city at an early age and became a shepherd. Meanwhile, at the wedding of Peleus and Thetis, Eris, the goddess of strife, threw into the congregation a golden apple inscribed with the words 'For the most beautiful'. The goddesses Hera, Athena and Aphrodite all claimed the apple, and so asked Zeus, king of the gods, to adjudicate. Unwilling to risk the wrath of the two goddesses he did not choose, Zeus elected to ask a mortal to be the judge. That mortal was Paris.

Paris found himself unable to decide between the three goddesses, so each of them offered him gifts if they chose her. Hera offered Paris great power, and the control of all Asia. Athena offered him the gift of wisdom, and great prowess in battle. Aphrodite offered him bodily perfection, and the love of the most beautiful woman in the world: Helen. Paris was a great lover, and so he selected Aphrodite and her gift. He then returned to Troy and, with the help of Aphrodite, he sailed with a fleet of ships to Menelaus's palace in Greece and kidnapped Helen.

Helen's suitors were all the most powerful men in Greece. When she selected Menelaus as her husband, her other suitors vowed to protect the couple and their marriage. Menelaus's brother Agamemnon rounded up these suitors – including the legendary warrior Achilles, and Odysseus, whose journey back from the Trojan War is told in the sequel to *The Iliad*, *The Odyssey*. Together they created a massive fleet of ships, which set sail to lay siege to Troy. But the sides were too evenly matched, and the war dragged on for ten years.

The final year of the war was the most eventful. Paris's brother Hector killed Patroclus, the friend of Achilles, in battle; Achilles took revenge by defeating Hector. Achilles was thought to be unbeatable. As a child his mother had submerged his body in the River Styx, the boundary of the Underworld, in order to confer immortality on him. But one part of the baby had been left dry: his heel. When Paris finally faced Achilles in combat he shot an arrow which, guided by Apollo, hit Achilles in the heel and killed him. Paris himself was later killed in battle.

It was Odysseus, who had been awarded the armour of Achilles as he was deemed to be the warrior most deserving of it, who came up with the plan that was to end the Trojan War. The Greeks built a huge wooden horse, inside which they hid their finest warriors. The Trojans saw the Greek ships sailing away, and believed that the horse was a peace offering which signified the end of the war. They brought it inside their gates and celebrated with a massive party. When they were deep in their cups, the Greeks crept out of the wooden horse, torched the city and recaptured Helen.

The massive task of adapting Homer's work, a cornerstone of Western literature, for the big screen was taken on by the acclaimed novelist and screenwriter David Benioff. It was a heavy duty for any writer, but Benioff was clear about the job ahead. 'I can't measure up to Homer,' he admitted. 'His composition has survived for nearly three millennia and remains the world's most beautiful and mournful depiction of war. But the story of the Trojan War does not belong to Homer. The characters he employs were legendary long before he was born. Dozens of different versions of the War have been told, and my script ransacks ideas from several of them. The script is not, truly, an adaptation of *The Iliad*. It is a retelling of the entire Trojan War story. So I'm not worried about desecrating a classic – Homer will survive Hollywood.'

Clearly the scope of the story was too vast to include in a single film, so Benioff had to make difficult decisions about what was to be cut out. The script that he ended up with was influenced by various other texts that included parts of the tale, including *The Odyssey*, Virgil's *Aeneid* and Ovid's *Metamorphoses*. In the film, the gods themselves do not have a

Paris's ships arrive to spirit away Helen.

part to play – their influence is acknowledged, but they do not appear. *Troy* is very much a film about human beings.

One of the aspects of the story of the Trojan War that makes it so enduring – and the perfect vehicle for actors to perform on screen – is the fact that this is not a clichéd story of good versus evil. In Hollywood terms its most recent sibling was *Gladiator*, but in many ways that was a very different kind of movie. Ridley Scott's Roman epic leaves us in no doubt as to where our sympathies lie: Maximus is good, Caesar is bad, and it's as simple as that. *The Iliad* is more subtle. All the characters are rounded, fallible human beings. None of them is entirely good, none of them

entirely bad. *The Iliad* is not black and white: it is shades of grey. This is what attracted Orlando to the crucial role of Paris.

'Paris is the anti-hero,' he explained. 'He's the young guy who's madly in love with Helen and he doesn't really realise the consequences. He's a lover, not a fighter. It's a real coming-of-age story for him, in terms of realising the folly of his deeds, having to live with losing a brother and his father, and seeing a city destroyed all because of his lust and love for a woman. It was interesting to me to try and find a way of playing that character. I don't want the audience to think, "What a despicable young man." So it was a challenge to find a human element to the character and make him somebody that an audience can understand as well as relate to in some way.'

And who better to play one of history's most famous lovers than Orlando Bloom? In terms of his status as a sex symbol, this was going to be the big one, not least because he was sharing the screen with the one actor who perhaps has set more hearts fluttering than any other: Brad Pitt. Even more so than Johnny Depp, co-starring with Pitt was perhaps the finest notch on Orlando's career bedpost.

Brad Pitt has been a heartthrob to millions since almost stealing the show in 1991's *Thelma & Louise*. Unfortunately, because he has been linked to a stream of beautiful women, including Gwyneth Paltrow and his current wife, Jennifer Aniston, his position as the world's leading sex symbol has sometimes eclipsed the fact that he is an extremely accomplished actor. He has been nominated for two Oscars for his contribution to *Snatch* and *Twelve Monkeys*, and perhaps his finest moment was opposite Morgan Freeman in the dark, gruesome thriller *Se7en*.

Although Orlando did not spend a great deal of time filming with Brad, he was clearly impressed by him. 'He's such a lovely man, and really an incredible actor. He's had a really fascinating career, and is a very handsome man, but very gracious and giving of his time and energy as well. He looks fantastic, and the role of Achilles is just so perfect for him.' Perfect indeed. Brad Pitt has always specialised in playing more complicated roles than his beefcake image would suggest, and Achilles is nothing if not complicated. In many ways he was the rock star of Ancient Greece, moody yet talented, and quirky – the legend has it that, in order to get out of honouring his promise to Menelaus, this ferocious warrior disguised himself as a woman.

It was while he was with Brad one day that Orlando got a taste of the level of fame that he knew might be not too far off for himself, and he was glad to see how the Hollywood superstar handled it. 'I was out with Brad in Malta. We walked out of the little tavern where we had some drinks and the flashbulbs exploded. He was swamped. He started a small riot. I turned to him and was like, "Aren't you a little worried, mate?" Brad whispered in my ear, "Just keep walking. Smile. Shake hands. And just keep walking."

'But he had a bodyguard with him. I mean,

'I'm not worried about desecrating a classic – Homer will survive Hollywood.'

DAVID BENIOFF, TROY SCREENWRITER

that's kind of intense when you need a bodyguard with you. That kind of wigs me out, to be honest. But I admired so much the way Brad had grace and composure in that moment. He had a bit of a wild look in his eye because obviously it was freaky. But he handled it really well.'

Eric Bana, star of *Chopper* and *The Hulk*, plays Paris's brother, Hector, in the film. It is assured casting – he and Orlando have similarities of features that make them convincing as siblings – and he evidently fell for

'Just keep walking,' Brad told Orlando as they were being mobbed by admiring fans. 'Smile. Shake hands. And just keep walking.'

Orlando's charm: 'He's an absolute sweetheart. Orlando is Orlando effortlessly. He just is. He's always very aware of what's going on around him, how people are being treated, how he's behaving.' It was a reassuring comment that showed that Orlando was not allowing the dizzy heights of his success to go to his head.

'He's an **absolute** sweetheart. Orlando is Orlando **effortlessly**. He **just** is.'

ERIC BANA ON ORLANDO BLOOM

As well as being wowed by Brad Pitt's level-headedness, and inspiring elegant character references from Eric Bana, Orlando once more found himself in the company of one of the elder statesmen of the acting world. Peter O'Toole has one of the most impressive lists of credits of any film actor – particularly for the remarkable *Lawrence of Arabia* – as well as having made a name for himself as one of the world's most accomplished stage performers. He is also well known for being a bit of a hell-raiser, relentlessly hard-drinking and a dedicated smoker. In *Troy* O'Toole took the part of Paris's father, King Priam, and Orlando was instantly transfixed by his rakish charm. 'He's a great raconteur,' said the younger actor.

'He's the sharpest wit I've ever met. This one time he's walking up these stairs with a fag hanging out of his mouth, and someone says to him, "Peter, have you ever thought of giving up cigarettes?" And he goes, "No, but I've thought about giving up stairs!" He's a very cool man.'

Orlando Bloom was armed with a bow and arrow; Brad Pitt was armed with a sword; director Wolfgang Petersen was armed with a budget of more than $150 million, and he intended to put it all up on the screen. He had had plenty of experience with massive budgets, his previous work as a director including the acclaimed U-boat movie *Das Boot* and *The Perfect Storm*. However, shooting did not go according to plan: the best-laid plans of this master film-maker were sent awry by what can only be described as two rather major strokes of irony. First, the supposedly impenetrable gates of Troy, constructed on location in Mexico, were utterly destroyed by Marty. Marty is not an actor or a member of the crew, but a hurricane, and Hurricane Marty achieved what the Greek hordes could not.

In addition, Brad Pitt suffered an injury that put him out of action for some time. Not even the twisted irony of the Greek gods could have come up with a more appropriate accident: during the filming of *Troy* he damaged his Achilles tendon...

CHAPTER NINE

KNIGHT RIDER

'DO I FEEL GRATEFUL TO BE AROUND
BEAUTIFUL WOMEN? OF COURSE I DO.
ALL GUYS LOVE BEAUTIFUL WOMEN.'

As the end of 2003 approached it was commented on that Orlando Bloom had spent an awful lot of his career brandishing either a sword or a bow and arrow – or both. Was he being typecast? Was being the goody-twoshoes action hero something that he intended to make a career out of? Certainly not – he is quite forceful about it. 'I've had enough of being the cool, clean-shaven elf, the cool, wholesome pirate slayer. Do I want to be a pin-up? Do I want to just be a poster boy? No I don't.' If he felt uncomfortable being a teenage heartthrob, it was something he was going to have to get used to. Suddenly more fan sites were being devoted to him than to Brad Pitt or Johnny Depp. *Tatler* magazine voted him Britain's most eligible bachelor, toppling even Prince William from the number-one spot. And there was scarcely a round-up of the world's top-ten most popular men that didn't include Orlando Bloom somewhere near the top. He even ranked number 12 in a list of the people with most influence on British culture.

As Orlando attended the various press launches for *The Return of the King*, fans desperate to catch a glimpse of their hero camped outside cinemas with banners emblazoned with the words 'Marry Me Orly!'; the thrill they received by getting just a glimpse of Orlando was almost Beatle-esque in its intensity. His co-star from *Pirates of the Caribbean*, Mackenzie Crook, put it in a nutshell: 'Orlando's an amazing babe magnet, the girls go absolutely crazy for him.' If the young star did not want to be a pin-up, he was going to be sorely disappointed.

In fairness to him, though, he had always made a point of trying to focus people's attention on his work rather than his personal life. This is not to say that he does not have a passion for the opposite sex – 'Do I feel grateful to be around beautiful women? Of course I do. All guys love beautiful women' – but from day one he has been conscious of the pressure constant media attention can have on the relationships of anyone in his situation. As a result, and following the lead of his mentor Johnny Depp, he has religiously kept certain things private; there are things he will talk about and things he won't, and he refuses to cross that line.

In fact, by the time he had become a bona fide global heartthrob, he had settled into a long-term relationship with the beautiful actress Kate Bosworth. Suddenly the inveterate gossiping stopped. (Had he had a fling with Keira Knightly? No. Naomi Watts? No. Is he gay? Come on!) While Orlando still constantly refused to comment on his relationship with Kate, it quickly became

'Do I feel grateful to be
around beautiful women?
Of course I do. All guys love
beautiful women.'

Hollywood's worst-kept secret, and he soon found himself acknowledging in interviews that they were an item.

Unlike Orlando, Kate had never really harboured dreams of being an actress. Born on 2 January 1983 in Los Angeles, she grew up in various different locations across America, including Connecticut and Massachusetts. At that time her principal passion in life was her horses, and she became a champion equestrian at an early age. More out of curiosity about the film industry than anything else, when she heard that Robert Redford was adapting the novel *The Horse Whisperer* for the big screen, she decided to audition. She did it largely for the experience – her previous acting had been limited to strictly amateur productions – and so was astonished when she landed a significant role in the movie.

But, much like Orlando when he landed his first feature-film role in *Wilde*, Kate kept a level head. After taking 18 months to complete her education and consider her options, she won herself a place at the University of Princeton. However, the lure of the cameras led to her deferring her further education when she was offered a role in the television series *The Young Americans*, and

Beautiful Kate Bosworth – the woman who is the envy of Orlando's fans around the world.

this was followed by the feature films *Remember the Titans* and *The Newcomers*. Her really big break, though, was to come with the romantic comedy *Blue Crush*, a surfing movie that was not universally praised, but which nevertheless put Kate's name well and truly on the map. She took a role in the adaptation of Bret Easton Ellis's novel *The Rules of Attraction* – and put her college place on hold yet again.

When Orlando flew Kate to Morocco during the filming of *Troy*, it was a titbit considered worthy of headline news in the celebrity gossip pages. And yet, for two people who had had such fame thrust on them in such a short period of time, they handled the attention with dignity and restraint. When rumours abounded that Orlando had proposed marriage, no comment came from the couple. They were determined that this relationship was not going to go the way of so many Hollywood pairings.

It was perhaps not surprising that the public perception of Orlando's roles was that he specialised in characters that required an outrageous costume and a sword. Legolas, Will Turner and Paris were parts that had brought him widespread recognition, but there is a flip side to every coin: these swashbuckling performances had been the making of him, but he was tired of the mistaken apprehension everybody seemed to have that he was being typecast. It was an apprehension not borne out by the facts: his career was marked by eclecticism, and films such as *Wilde*, *Ned Kelly* and *The Calcium Kid* showed that his dedication to producing a varied body of work was always at the forefront of his mind. Besides, this cocktail of characters had certainly done the arc of his career no harm to date. As he laid

> 'It's a **pretty intense** little film, both visually and **emotionally** and I think an **audience** will feel the **impact** of that.'
>
> ORLANDO BLOOM ON *HAVEN*

down his breastplate and bow and arrow at the end of the filming of *Troy*, he was in discussions about two films that would continue his varied biography in a similar vein – and give him a shot at playing the lead in one of the biggest pictures Hollywood had yet produced.

When *Troy* was in the can, Orlando left the dry heat of Morocco for the golden beaches of the Cayman Islands. South of Cuba, and west of Jamaica; these are well-known holiday hotspots, but Orlando was not on vacation. 'It hasn't been too much lying around on the beach,' he sighed when asked if he had had the opportunity to catch a few rays. He was returning to the Caribbean not as a pirate, but to film a movie a little less fantastical. *Haven* saw Orlando sharing the bill with Hollywood stalwarts Bill Paxton and Gabriel Byrne. It was also his first foray into the difficult and intricate world of movie production. Being a co-producer meant that the onus was on him to really make the movie work, and he spoke about the project with his characteristic enthusiasm. 'It's a pretty intense little film, both visually and emotionally and I think an audience will feel the impact of that. I play a young character called Shy who is a happy-go-lucky young British man who's been brought up in the Cayman Islands. He's in love with this young Caymanian girl; he's kind of from the wrong side of the tracks and she's from the right side of the tracks, and they get together to the fury and anger of their families.'

Byrne and Paxton play a pair of dodgy businessmen who, at risk of imprisonment by the American authorities, flee to the Cayman Islands. A complicated sequence of events leads to Orlando's character committing a crime that could change his adopted country for ever.

It's a million miles away from the genres Orlando had found himself becoming associated with, and that was just how he liked it. 'It's great to do a movie without a sword for once in a while,' he conceded, and the preparation for the movie could not have been more different from, say, *The Lord of the Rings*. In *Haven* he plays a fisherman; for this role, rather than having to learn how to ride horses and shoot objects out of the air with a bow and arrow, he simply went down to the docks and watched people fishing.

The challenge of being the movie's co-producer was one that he found added a whole new dimension to the experience. 'It's the first time I've done that. By getting involved in something you believe in, you can help forward a film. In terms of the role that I've been playing as a producer, it's been really just a sounding board; it's pretty much a collaborative effort, and we're all just mucking in and getting on with it.' It was a typically modest remark from a young man whom many film-makers would have given a great deal to have attached to one of their projects in any capacity. For Frank E. Flowers, *Haven*'s first-time writer and director, it must have seemed as though all his Christmases had come at once; for his part, Orlando put all his faith in the film-maker, praising the 'incredible energy and enthusiasm' he put into the project.

Up until now Orlando had managed to avoid courting controversy. Little did he know when he accepted it that his next picture would look set to disturb that balance.

Ridley Scott had had his eye on the young actor for some time now. He was supremely impressed with the performance he had given in *Black Hawk Down*, and had watched with almost paternal satisfaction as Orlando's star continued to rise. Towards the end of 2003, as Scott was beginning to put his next project into production, he considered that Orlando had now grown sufficiently as an actor for him to take his next step. To take the lead role in a multimillion-dollar Hollywood movie is a weighty task for even the most experienced actor – it is not for nothing that they command such high fees, and earn immense respect within the industry if they pull it off – and so the regard in which Scott held Orlando must have been considerable when he asked him to audition for the lead part in his new picture, *Kingdom of Heaven*.

It was back in the saddle for Orlando but, despite his claims that he wanted to do a few films that did not involve swords and horses, this was certainly not an opportunity he was going to miss. Quite the opposite – he admitted that when he got the call it sent shivers down his spine. He had always admired the director's work, and he cannot have been oblivious to the impact his last

95

historical epic, *Gladiator*, had had on the career of its star, Russell Crowe. He was also aware of the responsibility that was being laid on him. 'I'm really grateful to Ridley for giving me the opportunity, because I know he will make a great movie. I'm in the hands of a master. As long as I keep my end of the bargain, I know he's going to deliver, and I know *I* can deliver, so I hope it's going to come through. I think the star of the movie will be the way that he makes it. He's that kind of a guy, so I'm really glad that this is my first lead role.'

Kingdom of Heaven is set during the time of the Crusades. It takes place in and around Jerusalem and tells the story of a young peasant who becomes a knight in order to take up the defence of his city, and who falls in love with the princess. The young peasant is, of course, Orlando, and it is clear why the film-makers believed he was perfect for the role, with his ability to capture that sense of fresh-faced sincerity. But lest anyone should think that this was just Will Turner in armour, it was soon made clear that the movie was a good deal more complex than that. 'I wanted to do a film with knights in armour,' explained Scott, 'but thought, Why do some homogenous story when screenwriter William Monahan came up with such rich history? He based this drama on accurate

> '**I'm** really **grateful** to Ridley for giving me the **opportunity**, because I know he **will** make a great **movie**. I'm in the **hands** of a **master**.'
>
> ORLANDO BLOOM

research, which he spent 19 months compiling and writing.'

Ridley Scott and Orlando Bloom set out to make a sensational, epic love story which was firmly based in history. Their intentions were of the best, and they were keen to make sure that the movie was no less than a 'fascinating history lesson'; but it was here that the controversy surrounding *Kingdom of Heaven* arose. The film-makers made a decision to present the story of the Crusades from a Muslim perspective: a cross-cultural alliance of Christians, Muslims and Jews defend Jerusalem from the marauding Knights Templar. It was an approach which infuriated academics. It was nonsense, they declared, based on an outdated and romanticised version of history propagated by the novelist Sir Walter Scott in the 19th century. It was a misinterpretation of the facts that had been

Orlando Bloom – a man just doing what he loves.

perpetuated by Saddam Hussein and the former Syrian dictator Hafez Assad. This, they went as far as saying, was Osama bin Laden's version of history.

The director and his lead actor must have been perplexed by the hostility their project was provoking. They had set out in good faith to produce an entertaining movie based on historical fact, and had caused an outrage. They stuck to their guns, and, while Scott admitted that he was trying to portray the Arabs in a positive light, he added, 'It's trying to be fair, and we hope that the Muslim world sees the rectification of history. It's a serious look at the subject and the fascinating things about these two parallel religions which come into conflict. It is not a hack-and-thrust with a lot of sword fighting.'

Orlando was more robust in his defence of the movie's approach. 'It's not at all Hollywood's typical, action-orientated account of the Crusades. Ridley wanted it to be historically tenable. He even took the script and the storyboards to the Moroccan government to get an Islamic government's official seal of approval on the nature and content of the film. He wanted to tell the story without all the inaccuracies that would offend the Muslim world. It is amazing that such a successful film-maker can show such levels of humility.'

'I'm lucky to have been involved in some really big movies now and I'm a bit more comfortable on a big set. I know how it works.'

ORLANDO BLOOM

With the controversy continuing all around them, all the film-makers could do was what they did best: make films. Orlando got stuck into the project with his customary flair, acknowledging that the time he had spent on major projects over the past few years was going to be a huge help to him: 'I'm lucky to have been involved in some really big movies now and I'm a bit more comfortable on a big set. I know how it works.' In truth, he felt more at ease being cushioned by the lavishness of a big production than he did on the set of smaller movies he had made. 'A little film I've been working on [*Haven*], I was really anxious. I was really nervous about how I was going to be able to cope with it, but it's cool.' Well, if it was a big set he wanted, they don't come much bigger than this: Ridley Scott described the scale of the production as being larger even than *Gladiator*, and anyone who had seen his previous masterpiece knew that that was no mean claim. Would Orlando be able to pull it off? Only time would tell.

EPILOGUE

The evening of 13 January 2004. As filming finished, the sun slowly followed its course and dipped behind the Spanish mountains, leaving a balmy Mediterranean twilight in its wake.

For Orlando Bloom, as he walked off set on his twenty-seventh birthday, life was good. As the cast and crew presented him with a huge birthday cake – freshly baked in a local bakery – and a few bottles of the finest wine to wash it down with, he was able to reflect on the tumultuous events of the past five years. He had come a long way since, as an unknown drama student, one among thousands of hopefuls and wannabes, he had received the call asking him to audition for a movie about hobbits. Had he managed to cobble a living together playing bit parts on TV series, he would probably have been quite happy – his only ambition had been to succeed as a jobbing actor. Now his poster was on the walls of teenage girls all over the world. His face peered out from the pages of stylish magazines. He was dating one of the most beautiful actresses in the world. And the acting world was his oyster.

The future looked as rosy as the setting sun. He was signed up to reprise his role in another instalment of *Pirates of the Caribbean*; and, to show that it wasn't all swords and swashbuckling, he was taking the lead in Cameron Crowe's more down-to-earth drama *Elizabethtown*. Orlando had spoken in the past of his desire to reach a stage where he could choose the projects and the directors he wanted. That stage had come. One thing was certain – there would be no shortage of interesting, challenging roles for this young actor from Kent with a knack for lighting up the big screen.

Modesty is one of Orlando's key characteristics and so, as he celebrated that night under the Iberian stars, he probably did not reflect that, while fate had played a major hand in his success, his own choices and above all his level-headed outlook on life had gone a long way to allowing him to achieve his goals. He was a Hollywood A-lister, without the A-lister's arrogance. He was impossibly famous, yet possessed the humility of a man who understands that fame can leave as quickly as it arrives. He knew that if he played his cards right, he would soon be rich beyond the dreams of avarice; but money was never the reason why he got into this game in the first place.

Orlando Bloom was just doing what he loved.

filmography

Wilde (1994)
Director: Brian Gilbert
Producers: Marc Samuelson,
  Peter Samuelson
Writers: Richard Ellman (book);
  Julian Mitchell (screenplay)
Cast: Orlando Bloom   Rent boy
Stephen Fry   Oscar Wilde
Jude Law   Lord Alfred 'Bosie'
    Douglas
Vanessa Redgrave   Lady Speranza Wilde

*The Lord of the Rings: The Fellowship
  of the Ring* (2001)
Director: Peter Jackson
Producers: Peter Jackson, Barry M. Osbourne,
  Fran Walsh, Mark Ordesky
Writers: Peter Jackson, Fran Walsh,
  Philippa Boyens
Cast: Orlando Bloom   Legolas
Ian McKellen   Gandalf
Viggo Mortensen   Aragorn
Elijah Wood   Frodo
Sean Astin   Sam
Christopher Lee   Saruman

Black Hawk Down (2002)
Director: Ridley Scott
Producers: Jerry Bruckheimer, Ridley Scott
Writer: Ken Nolan
Cast: Orlando Bloom   Ranger Private 1st
    Class Todd Blackburn
Josh Hartnett   Ranger Staff
    Sergeant Matt
    Eversmann
Eric Bana   Delta Sergeant 1st
    Class Norm Hooten
Ewan McGregor   Ranger Specialist
    Danny Grimes
Jason Isaacs   Ranger Captain
    Mike Steele

The Lord of the Rings: The Two Towers (2002)
Director: Peter Jackson
Producers: Peter Jackson,
  Barry M. Osbourne, Fran Walsh, Mark Ordesky
Writers: Peter Jackson, Fran Walsh,
  Philippa Boyens
Cast: Orlando Bloom   Legolas
Ian McKellen   Gandalf
Viggo Mortensen   Aragorn
Elijah Wood   Frodo
Sean Astin   Sam
Christopher Lee   Saruman

101

Pirates of the Caribbean: Curse of the Black Pearl (2003)
Director: Gore Verbinski
Producer: Jerry Bruckheimer
Writers: Ted Elliott and Terry Rossio
Cast: Orlando Bloom — Will Turner
Johnny Depp — Captain Jack Sparrow
Geoffrey Rush — Captain Barbossa
Keira Knightly — Elizabeth Swann

Ned Kelly (2003/2004)
Director: Gregor Jordan
Producers: Endymion Films
Writer: John Michael
Cast: Orlando Bloom — Joe Byrne
Heath Ledger — Ned Kelly
Geoffrey Rush — Superintendent Hare
Naomi Watts — Julia Cook

The Lord of the Rings: The Return of the King (2003)
Director: Peter Jackson
Producers: Peter Jackson, Barry M. Osbourne, Fran Walsh, Mark Ordesky
Writers: Peter Jackson, Fran Walsh, Philippa Boyens
Cast: Orlando Bloom — Legolas
Ian McKellen — Gandalf
Viggo Mortensen — Aragorn
Elijah Wood — Frodo
Sean Astin — Sam

The Calcium Kid (2004)
Director: Alex de Rakoff
Producers: Working Title 2 Films
Writers: Raymond Friel and Derek Boyle
Cast: Orlando Bloom — Jimmy
Omid Djalili — Herbie Bush
Billie Piper — Angel
Michael Pena — Jose Mendez

Troy (2004)
Director: Wolfgang Petersen
Producers: Wolfgang Petersen, Gail Katz, Diana Rathbun
Writer: David Benioff
Cast: Orlando Bloom — Paris
Brad Pitt — Achilles
Eric Bana — Hector
Diane Kruger — Helen
Sean Bean — Odysseus

Haven (2004 tbc)
Director: Frank E. Flowers
Producers: Robbie Brenner, Bob Yari, Orlando Bloom, Aleen Keshishian, Kelli Konop
Writer: Frank E. Flowers
Cast: Orlando Bloom — Shy
Bill Paxton — tbc
Gabriel Byrne — tbc

Kingdom of Heaven (2005 tbc)
Director: Ridley Scott
Producers: Ridley Scott, Branko Lustig, Lisa Ellzey, Perry Needham
Writer: William Monahan
Cast: Orlando Bloom — Balian
Liam Neeson — Godfrey of Ibelin
Jeremy Irons — Tiberias
Eva Green — Sibyllia

Elizabethtown (2005 tbc)
Director: Cameron Crowe
Producers: Cameron Crowe, Tom Cruise, Paula Wagner
Writer: Cameron Crowe
Cast: Orlando Bloom — Drew Baylor
Kirsten Dunst — Claire Colburn
Susan Sarandon — Mrs Baylor